BACKBONE POWER

THE SCIENCE OF SAYING NO

DR. ANNE BROWN PhD, RNCS

Disclaimer

NOTE: The reading of this book does not establish a doctor/nurse-patient relationship between the reader and Dr. Brown. As discussed numerous times in this book, implementing declines, requests, and authentic conversations into your life requires a safe environment. A personal relationship with a competent therapist is required to successfully end people-pleasing.

This book does not substitute for professional, therapeutic or medical advice. The author and the publisher specifically disclaim any liability, loss, or risk, personal or otherwise, that might be incurred, directly or indirectly, through the use and application of any of the content of this book. All matters regarding your emotional health and that of your family require the medical/psychological consultation and supervision of a competent psychotherapist.

The names and identifying characteristics of the individuals referred to in examples in this book have been changed to protect their identity.

Library of Congress Control Number 2010913283

ISBN-13: 9781619619012
ISBN: 1619619016
First printing 2010

CONTENTS

ACKNOWLEDGEMENTS

I owe a special acknowledgment and thanks to my teacher, Dr. Fernando Flores, for his profound influence on my life and my work. I am extremely grateful to all of the teachers and students in my Ontological Design Community with Dr. Flores.

It is an honor for me to thank my adviser and mentor, Dr. Ray Dorritie, whose encouragement, guidance, and support from beginning to completion enabled me to have a better understanding of the project. I am truly indebted to him for his leadership.

Dr. Constance Clancy-Fisher, a devoted friend who is there every step of the way, thank you for your support and friendship.

Love and thanks to my dear friend Suzanne Farver, whose steadfast support, wisdom, laughter, and encouragement help me cross many finish lines, including and especially this book.

Hockmeyer Studios (Ann, Beth, and BC) with its exquisite care under the guidance of my talented brother Brian deserve a very special acknowledgment and thanks!

I am especially indebted to Ted Nickerson for his words of wisdom and delightful sense of humor, and for the title.

Thank you to my blessed children Whitney and Greg who have taught me so much. I am humbled by and grateful for the shoulders I stand on of those who have passed but are not forgotten: Gigi, Poppa, Aunt Roma, Dad, Mom, Charlie and Teo.

To Robyn Cruz Harrington, thank you for your devotion to this project.

I am deeply grateful to all my close friends, clients, and family who have supported this endeavor.

AUTHOR'S NOTE

Research tells us that the more we know about ourselves—and the more honest we are with ourselves and others, the more we speak authentically—the more successful we will be in our career, our love life, our family and health, and with our friends. If our speaking and actions are driven by honesty, we will be in the world with authenticity, power, passion, dignity, and peace.

People-pleasing is driven by distortion of the truth, avoidance of conflict, the need to be liked, insecurity, poor self-esteem, giving away power, etc. People-pleasers are taken advantage of by takers, addicts, bad boyfriends or girlfriends, predators, people driven by greed, etc. Because they cannot take care of themselves in the presence of these people, they often feel like victims in the world.

That world is smaller, complex, challenging, and darker, and we need skills to be able to negotiate our way through life. I have found that implementing three distinctions otherwise known as Backbone Tools can radically change one's life. These are: the ability to say No with dignity, make requests, and speak authentically.

All of us need Backbone Tools. When you bump up against the Bernie Madoffs of the world and they can't tolerate requests, it is time for you to move on before you find your wallet empty. The people in twelve-step programs can greatly enhance their recovery by being in a Backbone group and learning Backbone skills.

I believe that for most people who are struggling with addiction, including eating disorders, there is a component of people-pleasing. Women who have been abused, or are being abused, need to develop Backbone skills after they are in a safe environment. Those who learn these skills early in life will have the tools to avoid abusive, toxic situations. When we all meet the temptations of the world, we need the skills to assess whether these substances (alcohol and other drugs, unhealthy foods, unnecessary pills, etc.) are good for us or if we need to say No to them.

How did our obesity rate get to be so high? People are not saying No to unhealthy foods that are clearly designed to line the pockets of the companies making them, not to support your health. When we meet the unhealthy, toxic people of the world, we need to say No to allowing them access to us. When people try to brainwash us with lies, we need to have the tools to say No to their brainwashing.

The first order of business is to assess if your environment is safe. Can the people around you tolerate your becoming your own person? Can they support your truth? Again, the first order of business is to assess whether your environment is safe. If it isn't, there are organizations that can help you get out of an unsafe environment. Once you are in a safe place, start reading, get a group together, and start working.

Enjoy the journey. I, for one, did not arrive with a voice. I, like others, have learned the joy of living powerfully with dignity and authenticity through my journey. Many of the examples this book discusses are from my journey, which is ongoing. Once you are in a safe environment, embrace the learning, and let's get going.

FOREWORD

BY CONSTANCE CLANCY-FISHER, EdD

As you read this empowering book that Dr. Brown has so passionately written, it is obvious that we can no longer pretend that people-pleasers and addiction doesn't exist; it is prevalent. Most if not all of us know at least one individual who is suffering from an addiction, victimhood or martyrdom. It touches all of our lives in some way. Reality is, it won't go away without taking necessary action and standing up to those who are master's at sabotaging your own growth.

The Science of Saying No brings insight into waking up, making the decision to set an intention, and accept the challenge of learning to say NO, which means YES for you.

As you begin practicing your own self-care and gaining inner peace, you will come to the realization that you are the priority. Developing a backbone takes awareness, courage and inner strength. It is a process. Dr. Brown takes you step by step through this journey. You courageously explore and embrace these steps that take you to your own expansion and growth.

Consider how you would feel once you develop and use your backbone to gain the honor and respect you desire and are worthy of. Yes, you will be tested. That is part of the challenge. However, working through this journey brings you to the other side where self-respect and empowerment exist, and you won't be disappointed.

Journey with Dr. Brown and allow yourself to be open to your own inner guidance and intuition and use the power of your wise self that has been yours all along.

As a practicing therapist for the last twenty-five years, she gives you many tools and exercises to apply along your way. Now it's up to you to give yourself permission to expand your soul's reach and thrive. By healing yourself, you are healing the world, step by step, moment by moment.

Constance Clancy-Fisher, EdD
Psychotherapist, Author, *Surviving Stress with a Healing Heart*

INTRODUCTION

Babies are born with somewhere in the area of 100 billion brain cells. That's approximately half the number of stars in the Milky Way, and, in fact, a galaxy of stars isn't such a bad way of visualizing a baby's brain, because it accurately depicts the purity and innocence of a clean but unique, individualized slate. There are no relationships, good or bad, between the stars.

Now visualize connections between the stars, like charts of constellations. That's what happens when we, as babies, are exposed to life. The nature of our experiences influences the connections among our brain cells. These connections are known as synapses, and they help us make sense of the world around us.

Initially, that world consists of our immediate family, and as children, we do our damnedest to make sense of it. We observe, listen, adapt, and then accommodate. In dysfunctional families, however, as hard as the children of these families might try, it is impossible to accommodate everyone.

In these situations, we become breeding grounds for anxiety. We try to fix everything, which, of course, is impossible, but we're determined. No, we're desperate. We overcompensate and take on traits we wouldn't have otherwise. By the time we reach adulthood—even our teen years—those traits are magnified, and the truth is now turned on its head. We say Yes when we mean No. [1]

- *Yes to sex with the ex*

- *Yes to paying for things we can't afford*

- *Yes to things we know feel good at the time and cost us our self-esteem later*

- *Yes to numbing ourselves with food, alcohol, and drugs*

- *Yes to sex to be liked*

- *Yes to being sweet to parents and step-parents who treat us poorly*

- *Yes to abusive bosses*

- *Yes to our friends partying at our house when our parents are away*

- *Yes to oral sex that teenage boys want from us because we think we will be more popular*

- *Yes to unfair salaries*

- *Yes to "putting up with" and "doing more than others"*

- *Yes to any request from anyone because we want to avoid conflict*

Then we wonder why we feel controlled, bullied, used, and abused.

We help others but never ask for help in return. Our Saturday plans to have fun find us doing yet another something else for someone else. Time and time again, we accept the short end of the stick. We curse ourselves for having partners who won't commit, partners to whom we're nicer and nicer, for whom we keep making sacrifices, who we support in their world with no reciprocation, for whom we buy things we can't afford, until one day, our partner has moved on and found someone else. We feel used and discarded while our partner already has the new relationship. But we were so nice.

Or we give and give, expecting our partners to do the same, and when they don't, we leave because we are so filled with resentment that we feel entitled to leave. We gave so much, and our partner gave so little. We keep score, and we always come out giving more—the victim.

We look in the mirror and see failure—again. Yet all we did was give and give. Resentment rears its ugly head. Our families refuse to see our newfound success as adults and treat us like the black sheep we were while growing up. They continue to manipulate us the way they did when we were the babies of the family growing up. Our friends are addicts and manipulate us, too. How is it that we can manage a successful business but still have a failed personal life?

In thirty years of practicing psychotherapy, these have been some of the stories of my patients. In every case, there is a common thread: the adaptive skill of trying to please everyone. In a world that is complicated and not always friendly, people-pleasing usually has devastating results. [2]

People-pleasers are at risk in the domains of finances, love, sex, family, and friendship. How many times have you shorted yourself financially, for example, because you were unwilling to request what you deserved? How many times have you said Yes to sex when you wanted to say No? How many times have you wanted to walk with dignity only to hold your head in shame or as a victim?

Warriors, by contrast, set boundaries, request what they need, and are comfortable saying No. The Indians in Dances With Wolves are excellent examples. In their world, honesty wasn't rewarded, nor was dishonesty frowned upon; instead, honest communication seemed to be the only form they knew.

If you haven't seen the movie, you should. It's an epic example of two cultures clashing—those of the Sioux and the European settlers. The settlers slaughter Indian men, women, and children with the same disregard they do animals. One scene is particularly demonstrative. It shows a traumatized buffalo calf wailing among a field of countless dead and skinned buffalo killed only for their hides.

By contrast, the Sioux are also portrayed hunting buffalo, but they kill as few as possible, only what they can eat and use completely. A celebration follows the hunt.

There was an undercurrent to everything they did that emphasized dignity. Confrontations, for example, were resolved in a way that allowed all parties to retain their dignity, even the most relatively minor ones—like who would keep John Dunbar's lost hat.

The scene, if you recall, is a feast celebrating a successful buffalo hunt, during which Lieutenant Dunbar, played by Kevin Costner, notices that a large Sioux man has his hat.

> **Dunbar:** That's my hat.... That's my hat!

> **Big Warrior:** I found it on the prairie. It's mine.

> **Wind in His Hair:** The hat belongs to the lieutenant.

> **Big Warrior:** He left it on the prairie. He didn't want it.

Wind in His Hair: Well, you can see he wants it now.

We all know it's a soldier's hat. We all know who wears it. If you want to keep it, that's fine, but give something for it.

The Sioux warrior removes his knife and sheath from his belt and gives it to Dunbar.

Wind in His Hair: Good trade. [3]

On the other hand, the character Jenny in Forrest Gump, is an excellent example of a people-pleaser: good, kind, nice, thoughtful, caring, sensitive—and always getting the short end of the stick.

The childhood victim of an abusive father, Jenny as an adult has sex she doesn't want, lets men hit her, and finally contemplates suicide. Once she acknowledges her past, however, she begins to speak authentically and finds inner peace. As one of my clients so perfectly put it after undergoing a similar transformation, Jenny "left behind her angry, defensive way of thinking."

Jenny's transformation occurs when she returns to the house in which she grew up. She and Forrest are walking along a dirt road when they approach a dilapidated, deserted house. Jenny's entire demeanor changes, and she starts throwing rocks and anything else she can find at the house. One of her throws breaks a window, and Jenny falls to the ground Crying. Forrest kneels down next to her. Sometimes, he says, I guess there just aren't enough rocks. [4]

In today's world, it's no longer optional but mandatory to learn the skills of a warrior, and there are ways to go about it that don't require us to break windows, live in a teepee or join an ancient Japanese samurai sect. Today's warrior is a Life Warrior, and the process of becoming one entails learning three skills:

1) *How to say No*
2) *How to make requests* [5]
3) *How to speak authentically* [6]

As you begin, of course, there will be fear. Fear is a normal part of change. So are awkwardness and self-doubt. Embrace them, as they signify your first steps toward becoming a warrior. No one is born with a warrior spirit, and everyone who has set out to make it a part of their lives initially felt the same fears you will. Declare yourself a beginner, and give yourself permission to make mistakes.

If you do, you'll soon find yourself on the road to dignified and authentic living. Along the way, you just may double your income, end toxic relationships, and raise healthier children. Right from the start, you'll notice a difference. Just learning to say No comes with all sorts of positive change.

CHAPTER ONE

OVERVIEW

As anxious as you are to begin learning How to Say No, and as anxious as I am for you to begin to see and feel the results, let's first see what's at stake.

If people-pleasing amounted to nothing more than a series of misguided choices, we could simply add, "Correct them" to our To-Do list. But that's not the case.

The consequences of people-pleasing are severe, and cost us in the domains of health, personal life, finance, relationships, career, and dignity, much like any serious illness. [7]

If you learned you had cancer, you would drop everything to seek treatment. While people-pleasing doesn't carry the same stigma as the C-word, it does come with serious consequences of its own, and requires immediate attention.

So what is this phenomenon of people-pleasing? In essence, it's the need to avoid conflict and make everyone in the world like us. It's an irrational goal that comes with all kinds of serious risks to our emotional and physical well-being.

Emotional Health Risks

Instead of engaging in healthy and relaxing conversation, people-pleasers put themselves through an emotionally exhausting process. Take the following conversation:

> **Landlord:** "You're the worst tenant I've ever had. You make too much noise. I can hear you upstairs. I can hear you in the bathroom. I can hear you on the phone. The lights are always on. I can see them through the crack

under the door. You're always washing your clothes. You're costing me a fortune."

Tenant: ....

Why can't the tenant respond right away? Because for years, he's suppressed his own ideas. The longer we play the role of people-pleaser, the less likely it is that we know how we feel about anything anymore.

Instead, we revert to behavior we acquired as children, when we did our best to keep dysfunction at bay: parents yelling, hitting, drinking, bullying, intimidating, and/or disappearing.

Before we respond to someone like the landlord, people-pleasers process a series of thoughts:

- *What can I say to ensure that I'll be liked?*

- *What's troubling the other person? (This is otherwise known as mind reading.)*

- *How do I phrase my response so as to avoid any confrontation?*

Then and only then, after having completed this exhausting mental exercise, with what profound and poignant words do we respond?

Tenant: Yes, you're right.

What's even more disappointing is that, in all likelihood, we actually believe it. After all, everyone in our family always told us how horrible we were. Maybe it's true.

Client: Maybe my landlord is right. Everyone in my family told me I was thoughtless, noisy, clumsy, insensitive, and a burden, so it must be true. I've been trying to live quietly in her house, but I guess I'm just incapable.

Therapist: No. Actually, when you pay rent to someone, you have the right to create yourself in that space. You are not horrible! This is simply a toxic environment for you.

It took some time for this client to believe he was not the bad person here. Eventually, he moved out to create his own space with a gracious landlord.

If we're insecure and bullied by toxic people, the tendency is to blame ourselves. But how do we tell a toxic environment from a non-toxic one?

Setting Standards

It has to do with setting standards for ourselves and how we'll be treated. First, we have to be able to recognize when we lack such standards.

Those moments are often epiphanies, highly charged and emotional because they're simultaneously happy and sad. They are the very sorts of memories that when I open my office door each morning, I recall with delight.

I see myself sitting across from a client. He is on a couch; I'm in my chair. There's a coffee table between us, a bowl of chocolates, water, cough drops, certificates hanging on brick walls painted white.

> **Client:** I see what you're saying. I've never had standards for the way people can treat me.

In addition to recognizing that many of us don't have standards, if we're in an environment where standards we set are not honored, it's toxic.

What the domain is doesn't matter: love, health, finances, community service, parents, children. Nor does it matter who the other person involved is. Standards are standards.

For example, many of us accept ill-mannered treatment from a doctor or lawyer because of the status we give that person's job.

In fact, there's a TV commercial dealing with this point: A couple is sitting across from each other at a restaurant, menus in hand. A waiter approaches to take their order:

> **Waiter:** So, do you have any questions?

> **Woman:** What is the soup of the day?

> **Waiter:** We have a mulligatawny soup.

> **Woman:** Do you have any specials?

Waiter: We have a steak special today.

Woman: Oh, how is that cooked?

Waiter: It's pan-seared and then ....

Woman (interrupting the waiter): Does that come with a side dish? Is it grilled? Can I have it steamed? What do you recommend? What kind of pie do you have? Are you an actor? Aren't you from Ohio?

The woman won't let up. She's in an environment where she's comfortable, and it shows. She's comfortable asking questions.

Then the scene switches to the same woman alone with her doctor in his office, sitting on his examination table. The doctor has just finished telling her the diagnosis.

Doctor: Any questions?

Woman: ....

She's about to ask a question but instead shakes her head, then waves the doctor away. Clearly, she's out of her comfort zone. The narrator takes over.

Narrator: Ask questions. Questions are the answer.

The ad is sponsored by the federal Agency for Healthcare Research and Quality and the U.S. Department of Health and Human Services. Its point, of course, is that we shouldn't feel intimidated, nor should we feel as if we're being difficult. In short, it's OK to question.

Of course, the higher our standards, the more likely it is that we'll find ourselves in conflict with others. Likewise, the lower our standards, the less likely there'll be conflict.

Yet the need to avoid conflict is the most common thread among people-pleasers. You can see the conundrum. If we lower our standards and try to please everyone, we raise the likelihood that there will be consequences:

- *Lack of self-confidence*
- *Judgmentalism*
- *Anxiety*
- *Lack of self-knowledge*

- *Physical danger*
- *Depression*
- *Lack of Self-Confidence*

People-pleasing elevates others to a place of power and fuels their self-confidence. In turn, where does that leave us?

We revert to our childhood, when we hid our needs and desires from maladaptive parents unwilling to acknowledge us as anything more than a burden, people who seemed hell-bent on compromising whatever beauties and abilities we may have been blessed with. Our self-confidence wilts [8].

> **Client:** Every time I told my parents what was important to me, they'd say no. I wanted to play soccer. They made me do debate. I wanted to be in 4-H. They made me do track. Eventually, I stopped asking.

In many cases, parents like these weren't just controlling but hurtful as well.

> **Client:** I'm terrified to make requests. All it does is give the other person information to hurt you with.

> **Therapist:** No matter what damage was done to us as children, we must give ourselves permission to share our needs, desires, and opinions. What we need to do is pick people to be in our lives who will honor those needs, desires, and opinions [9].

> **Client:** I've buried my needs with mental cartwheels so I could convince myself I didn't have any. It's scary as a child to know your needs won't be met. It's even scarier to have someone hurt you with the information you gave them because you thought they would take care of you. Now, I'm at the point where I feel like I've risen above having any needs. I can take anything anyone can dish out, and I never ask myself how I feel about what is happening.

By adulthood, people-pleasers often become arrogant about how accommodating and "nice" they are, compared with other people who are more "difficult."

Judgmentalism

People-pleasing fuels our judgmental side. In fact, there is a direct relationship between the degree to which we people-please and the judgments we make about others.

In our desire to avoid conflict, it's easier, of course, to pass judgment than it is to confront a person or situation directly. But that's not the way of the warrior. Imagine if the Sioux had had hair salons, therapists, and telephones:

> **Client:** I hate what my hairdresser did. Look at it. I don't know what to do. The color is horrible. I look like a trollop. Actually, I do know what to do. I told everyone what a horrible job she did, and to never use her.

> **Therapist:** What about calling the hairdresser? Hi, this is Wind in Her Hair, and, well, you colored my hair the other day, and I've tried living with it, but I'm just not happy with the results. I was wondering if we could discuss ways to make it look more like what I had in mind, something less trollopy.

> **Hairdresser:** Yes, come in this afternoon, and let's talk about how to fix it.

When we go to the source of our upset, we speak authentically and honestly. Of course, in real life, your hairdresser may very well tell you, "Too bad," in which case you simply don't go back.

You are not an awful person because you registered your upset. Remember, you can only make the request. You cannot control its outcome. But you've got to make that request. Otherwise, you'll just build up resentment, and that, in turn, will lead to being overly judgmental.

> **Client:** I just found out my new boyfriend can't come up with his share of the rent. I swear, this is the story of my life. Everyone I've talked to says we're moving too fast and he's just using me. I just think about him and I get that gnawing feeling of resentment.

> **Therapist:** Who do you need to have this conversation with, other than "everyone"?

Client: I need to talk to my boyfriend. But what if he can't? What if he won't? What if he gets upset with me?

Therapist: Who's upset now?

Client: Me.

Therapist: So why is it standard operating procedure for you to be upset with the people you see taking advantage of you and yet you're terrified to upset them?

Client: It's like a double standard. I'll take whatever someone dishes out, but I can't handle the idea of upsetting that certain someone. What is that about?

Therapist: At the risk of sounding like a therapist, I'm going to speculate that:

1) Confrontation was scary for you as a child.
2) You're accustomed to getting the short end of the stick.
3) The victim role is one you've not only become accustomed to but also one that actually brings a level of comfort.

Let's see what will happen if you go to your boyfriend and let him know how you feel. What do you think you'll be able to say to him? [10]

> **Client:** I want to work out an agreement that won't lead me to feel resentful, so I need to figure out what it is I want from him in the area of money and chores, things like that.

> **Therapist:** Sounds good.

Here's the following week's session:

> **Client:** I drew up a contract with a list of all the things he's responsible for and all the things I'm responsible for. I feel great. In the past, I'd have let this unfairness go on forever because "life wasn't fair to me as a child." I realized that a big part of my identity with people is how unfair life is for me.

Drawing up this contract took one hour. We both agreed, and now, we both feel great. I'm starting this relationship with no resentment, which is a first. I can see myself starting to say No to my legacy of people who take advantage of me, which just leads to my feeling used.

Therapist: You're right. We can help you become a warrior. Have you seen the movie Dances With Wolves? [11]

Anxiety

People-pleasing creates anxiety. Since we've only told people what we think they want to hear, there is anxiety about trying to remember what we've told everyone.

Then there's anxiety about not telling the truth, and the possibility of being found out.

And there's anxiety about ultimately hurting someone—or everyone, for that matter—if and when the truth is finally exposed.

Seven-year-old Julie tells her mom: I don't want Alison to spend the night. She's so bossy. (Alison's mom tends to look for babysitting from people-pleasing moms).

Julie's mom: OK, honey.

The next day, Alison's mom says to Julie's mom: I was so hoping Alison could spend tonight with Julie at your home. She's been begging me all day.

Julie's mom: Sure, of course.

(At the moment Julie's mom is trying to please Alison's mom, she really may not remember her promise to her own daughter).

Julie, upon finding out: "Mom, why can't you stand up to Alison's mom?"

Julie's mom, to herself: Good question.

Here's what happens in the therapist's office:

Client (Julie's mom): I made a mess, and my daughter is upset with me. What can I do now?

Therapist: Take a deep breath, call Alison's mom, and say, I made a mistake. Thank you for asking about the overnight, but it's not going to work for us to have Alison spend the night. (And be firm even if Alison's mom comes back with, "But she's made plans; what is she going to do?") Then apologize to Julie.

Client: I'm starting to see how if I don't have boundaries for myself, I can't properly care for the people I love.

Depression

The greatest tragedy that people-pleasers experience is the absence of any authentic relationship with themselves. The result is an ill-defined person, someone without a strong sense of self. Here's an example from one end of the spectrum:

When I was working as the evening charge nurse at an inpatient psychiatric unit, we admitted a woman suffering from depression. She told us horror story after horror story about how abusively her family had treated her.

When we explained how visitation worked, we let her know that she could veto anyone's visitation privileges. She decided to ban her family from visiting.

To our dismay, however, we watched her become more and more depressed, to the point of becoming suicidal. As bad as her family members were, without them, she felt worse. [12]

The role this patient had always played was that of the victim: "Look how poorly I'm being treated." But as bad as it is having the identity of the victim, it can feel better than having no identity at all.

Lack of Self Knowledge

We require identity and self-knowledge, or at least the perception of it. On the opposite end of the spectrum, many people-pleasers are very competent "out in the world," and are able to take on the identity of "success," in spite of the fact that they struggle to have success in their personal lives.

Client: When I'm on my own at home, I feel totally ungrounded. I'm depressed, unmotivated. When I'm at work, I've got direction.

Those around him determine this man's sense of self. When he's at work, he's one person. When he's at home, he's another.

As a child, it was the same. Outside his home, he was the best athlete, best student, great friend, etc. But at home, he was constantly criticized, shamed, and beaten down—the black sheep of the family. He taught himself to overachieve in the outside world and people-please the bad guys at home! Unfortunately, he may not believe he can be successful without a toxic home.

When we do not develop our authentic selves, or if we we're never given the opportunity to do so, we may also settle for toxic situations. Why? Because it's better than being alone, or we believe we need these situations.

We can get by as long as there are other people around. In fact, we may even overachieve at work and in social settings. In the case of this particular client, he continued his legacy of abuse at home with one critical, cold, and controlling relationship after another.

The people-pleasing, always-accommodating, victimized son became the people-pleasing, always-accommodating, victimized boyfriend, and ultimately, the people-pleasing, always-accommodating, victimized husband.

The reality is that as he continues to feed his poor self-esteem in this way, emotionally, he's more like the woman on suicide watch at the psychiatric unit, despite his highly successful career.

While we can survive with nothing more than the perception of a sense of identity, in order to thrive, we require the real deal. We need to take the time to understand who we are, what we believe, and what is important to us, etc.

Homework

Spend time on your own to develop an inner, private life. Find a belief system bigger than yourself, like nature, religion, or spirituality. Develop a practice such as meditation, yoga, prayer, exercise, deep breathing, anything that grounds you. [13]

It doesn't matter what it is as long as it does this in some way and lets you address some of life's big questions, like:

- *Who are you?*

- *What do you believe?*

- *How does the world work?*

- *Why do bad things happen to good people?*

- *What should you do when bad things happen to you?*

When the proverbial you-know-what hits the fan, you will be ready. You will have a reserve of emotional strength. You will be grounded, a warrior ready for action.

Although many people use addictions during times of crisis, addictions do not and should not qualify as grounding practices.

On the other hand, if you believe there is something bigger than you, and if you develop practices to support your relationship to whatever that is for you, then you never have to feel alone in the world.

Some people even prefer a spiritual base to having a partner, while others need that partner.

> **Client:** I have a good person in my life, and I'm practicing setting healthy boundaries. The person isn't critical and cold, which is a first for me, and I'm standing up for myself, which is also a first.

Practically speaking, this relationship is premature for this person, but he felt he simply could not continue to live alone. Nevertheless, though, he's practicing new behaviors and learning, and while it's not the ideal situation for self-improvement, it's not a detriment either.

We were able to fashion his experience with his new partner in such a way that it not only benefited my client but also allowed his partner to see individual growth in directions she was hoping to take too.

Unfortunately, however, the need to be with a partner sometimes trumps everything else, even the relationship with one's therapist. I've had clients who rather than leave a bad relationship, opted to leave therapy instead.

Fortunately, on occasion, they return.

> **Client:** He was married. I knew I needed to get out of being a married man's girlfriend. But I just wasn't ready. I was dreading our sessions. I'd see them in my Day-Timer and instead of looking forward to them, they were only a constant reminder of what I knew I needed to do. But I wasn't ready.

Homework

Sometimes, it's OK to put off change—temporarily. If you find yourself complaining about the same situation over and over and yet you can't leave, it may not be time to leave. But it may very well be time to stop complaining. Your friends are probably tired of hearing about it.

You are choosing to stay by choosing not to leave, so ask yourself, what is the learning for me? While it may not sound like it, there is opportunity to make the most of it even when you're stuck. Make it work for you. Sometimes, you need to build your self-confidence and get your ducks in a row before you leave.

> **Client:** I know my fears, and I get so tired of hearing myself complain—about the relationship, the drama, my own pathetic inability to change it. I see where my stubborn loyalty keeps getting me in trouble. I'm not blind to the abuse, and I'm not blind to the self-sabotage. It's just that staying with the familiar is less scary than braving the unknown. But now I'm ready.

Physical Dangers

Sorry to be the bearer of bad news—and sorrier still if you already knew this from first-hand experience—but people-pleasers are not equipped to deal with life's darker challenges:

- *Abusive relationships*

- *Child molestation*

- *Internet predation*

- *Rape*

- *Kidnapping*

It is difficult to determine the prevalence of abuse because definitions differ, and there are so many places where abuse can take place, e.g., families, workplace, elder care, churches, schools, child-care facilities, etc. But I think it is important to understand that it is far more prevalent than we would like to believe.

Each year, 1 million children in North America are confirmed as victims of child abuse or neglect, and over 1,200 die as a result of parental mistreatment. Overall, the reported rate of child abuse has increased by more than 300 percent since 1976. [14]

In addition, it is clear that the Internet facilitates pedophilic activity by providing anonymity, convenience, ability to organize, and access to victims. [15]

The U. S. Bureau of Justice Statistics reports that 75.6% of rapes were committed by persons known to the victim. [16]

Abusive Relationships

If you are already involved in a physically abusive relationship, there is no choice but to leave. If there were other choices, I would tell you. There are not. Do not make excuses. Do not think it will stop. Do not blame yourself. Leave! If your abuser is under the influence of drugs and alcohol, do not rationalize. Leave! If he is remorseful, apologizes, and says it will never happen again, Leave!

It is much easier if you leave the first time the abuse happens, but it is always better late than never. It is rare that someone who hits once will never hit again. Likewise, it is rare that someone who hits is not already being verbally and emotionally abusive.

People-pleasers are ideal prey for abusers. Who better for an abuser to seek out than the well-meaning person who:

- *Wants everyone to like her*

- *Never stands up for herself*

• *Lacks self-esteem*

• *Transfers power away from herself each time she's engaged in conversation*

Once their intuitive checklist is complete and they've set their sights on a victim, abusers know exactly how to trap their victim and keep her trapped. That's when the emotional abuse begins.

"No one would ever have you."

"I see your diet isn't working."

"You can't cook, you can't keep house, and you're a lousy mother."

"You're lucky I put up with you. No one else would have you."

"You want too much."

"I never realized how dumb you are."

"You're the reason I didn't get the job. You embarrass me."

"You're lucky to have me."

With his victim fully questioning her own self-worth, the abuser can get away with anything.

Client: My husband is cheating on me. We're pretending to be this happy family, and I'm dying inside. I feel like I'm going crazy.

Therapist: Is this the first time?

Client: No, it's the third, at least that I know of, and each time, he begged me to stay and swore it would never happen again. Now, I wonder if it will ever stop.

Therapist: Why do you think you stay?

Client: I don't know.

Therapist: Does he subtly put you down, saying things like:

• *You're so lucky to have me;*

> • *You'll never find anyone else;*
>
> • *No one will ever put up with you;*
>
> • *I'm the best thing that ever happened to you!*

Client: How did you know? Now that you say that, he always says he is the best thing that ever happened to me and that no one will ever have me.

Therapist: You offer a great companion for someone. You are bright, attractive, kind, a fabulous mother, a devoted wife, loved by the community, and you are being brainwashed to think otherwise by a subtle form of abuse.

Unfortunately, I don't know how this particular woman fared, as her husband moved the family. It's all too typical, this kind of geographical shift. Ripe with the hope of a fresh start, the family packs up its belongings—along with all its dysfunction—and moves them somewhere else.

Is That It?

Are there alternatives to leaving an abusive relationship? Is it always so cut and dried? You're hit, you leave, no questions.

When I was in Bali, I interviewed a lovely working mother and wife, and we discussed her family and values. She spoke of a family that had a strong spiritual base with daily prayer practices, authentic conversations between husband and wife, co-parenting, and mutual decision-making—overall, a family that I believed was operating with dignity.

I asked her what would happen if her husband hit her. "It depends on the circumstances," she replied instantly, "if he lost his job, or something horrible happened to someone in his family, like a death. It would depend on what was going on."

Now, I don't support hitting, and neither did she. If the behavior was an isolated incident, everyone understood that it still was unacceptable, and her partner was willing to talk about how to better deal with his feelings, then a strong family could heal from this deviant behavior.

Child Molestation

On February 8, 2010, Oprah Winfrey interviewed four child molesters with their therapist. I highly recommend this show for everyone, and particularly for parents. Child molesters look for vulnerable, needy children who are afraid to speak up, who need attention, and whose parents are absent or in denial.

Ninety percent of child molesters are known to the victim and the family. Child molesters do not want a feisty, confident child who will "rat" on them. Nor do they want parents who will believe their child. The pain of having a parent who doesn't believe you if you have the courage to speak up is almost insurmountable. Heads up! [17]

Internet Predation

People-pleasing patterns are often established early in life, but, of course, life offers plenty of opportunities to reinforce those patterns. Take teen dating, for example, and its greatest cost: the drama-based, limited discourse that accompanies "serious" dating at this young age.

Teen-dating conversations are about "hooking up," who slept with whose best friend, oral sex, lying to parents, unchaperoned parties, and secret meetings, all intended to please boys and gain popularity.

On the other hand, a better way to build self-esteem during one's teen years is to participate in activities like arts, music, sports, politics, and travel, which can teach about the world and help teens develop competences.

It is also a good time to build solid friendships without sex and conversations that revolve around sex. Teens who follow this path are better prepared and have more confidence, wisdom, and seasoning when they do date. And they also have a better chance of developing the self-esteem needed to see through and stand up to Internet predators, who look for people with poor self-esteem, a desire to accommodate, a need for validation, and the inability to say No.

Internet predators know how to say all the right things, to which the all-too-common teen response is, "Finally, someone understands me."

No, it's more like, "someone is about to take advantage of you."

When young daughters grow up in very strict, rigid, and highly disciplined, pious, righteous families, it can make their teen years a challenge, to say the least. The teen years are tough enough. When our parents' expectations are impossible to meet, they become that much tougher. As teens, we want—no, we need—to experiment, try new things, and test out our ideas about life. We need a strong and flexible family environment that allows for some playing room.

When our family doesn't understand the importance of a little latitude, one of two things will often result:

> • *We rebel*

> • *We become compliant. (And what is compliance, if not a form of people-pleasing?)*

Neither response is desirable, and each comes with consequences. Enter the Internet predator.

This type of person can make mincemeat of either type of teen, the rebel or the people-pleaser. For the rebel, the predator provides a means for acting out. Of course, unbeknown to the teen, the predator is just as controlling as her family.

As for the people-pleaser, the predator is just another person to whom she doesn't have the backbone to say No. What's more, as we've seen, people-pleasers, by default, transfer power whenever they engage in conversation.

All this makes an easy feast for the predator who, after some seductive talking, proposes an opportunity to meet—and the rest, of course, becomes material for news anchors and statisticians.

The seduction, it should be pointed out, can take almost any form. It doesn't even always have to be a male predator appealing to a rebellious teen, for instance.

We know only too well the story of the thirteen-year-old girl who committed suicide as a result of the predacious mom down the street who was bullying her on the Internet.

How were you raised? How are you raising your children now? If we don't do some work on ourselves, we are destined to recreate history.

As children introduced to the darker side of humanity, we cannot help but try to find a way to cope, and it is imperative that, as adults, we develop an understanding of:

- *What we had to cope with growing up*

- *What behaviors we adopted in order to cope*

- *What new tools we need to negotiate our way through life*

More times than not, my clients developed people-pleasing as a coping mechanism, and the new tools they used to successfully negotiate their way through life were those of the warrior, the abilities to:

- *Say No*

- *Make requests*

- *Speak authentically*

Kidnapping and Rape

The feminist theory of rape is male dominance over women, and an act of abusive power to dominate them. In this country, we women have legal rights that can protect us from physical dominance. But having the presence, energy, and mindset of a warrior is no guarantee you will not be raped, and it is counter to the victim mentality of being dominated by a male. [18]

Kidnappers, too, are more prone to release someone who makes their life miserable by fighting back.

I learned the hard way that we cannot always count on our bodies to react in ways that will protect us if and when we are threatened. I unconsciously chose checking out and amnesia when I was mugged years ago.

On the other hand, a friend of mine who was accosted in a parking garage grabbed her umbrella, growled ferociously, and went after her attacker, who fled.

Having warrior energy is not a guarantee you won't be the victim of a crime. But a strong body that carries itself with dignity, combined with strong conversations that support our dignity, can have a powerful presence in the world.

Takers

People-pleasers aren't at risk only from predators. Takers of any sort seek out people-pleaser profiles.

Addicts, for example, are the quintessential takers, and they can "smell" people-pleasers the way sharks can smell a drop of blood—from a mile away. Often, however, those addicts are closer to home. In fact, typically, they are people we love and care about deeply.

It has been particularly noteworthy in my practice just how many clients I've worked with on overcoming people-pleasing have addicts in their lives. It's noteworthy but not surprising.

We've all heard of Tough Love, and it is, in fact, one of the recommended ways to help addicts. People-pleasers, though, have a challenging time with the "tough" part of the package, and as a result, serve only to enable the addict's behavior.

The parents of one very-tough-to-treat addict wrestled with this concept continually. Sometimes, the husband would send his lovely wife in to confess his latest sin, e.g., new car for the poorly recovering addict, increase in allowance for the poorly recovering addict, etc. But in spite of the family's slips, the addict with her addiction, and the parents with their enabling, they all have healthier relationships now as they walk down the path of a family in recovery. What they lacked in "tough," they more than made up for with love, perseverance, detachment, unity, loyalty, and belief!

Another mother, of a young man from a wealthy family who was facing his twelfth DUI, paused for a moment when I asked her:

"When your son gets his thirteenth DUI, can the family not send lawyers to get him off the charges?"

"No," she said, "someone will call his lawyer to get him out of trouble."

"He knows that, so he has no reason to stop drinking," I replied.

The road for both the addict and the enabler is long and bumpy.

It's a bitter irony that the person who only wants to avoid conflict—the people-pleaser—can do so much damage to those she loves most. It's not just the addicts in her life who are put at increased risk; it's her spouse and children, too.

Our Relationships

Client: I want to divorce my husband. He's cold. He doesn't talk to me. All he does is work, and if he's not working, he's playing golf. The kids are not close to him— he's so strict.

Therapist: Have you brought these concerns up with your husband?

Client: Oh no, I could never do that.

Therapist: There will be no divorce under this roof until you start talking to your husband. You need to learn to speak up, and he needs to be able to fight for his marriage.

One of the most damaging emotional traumas is to deprive one's partner of the right to fight for his marriage.

When we tell our spouse only what we think he wants to hear, when we are always nice and accommodating, we build up a long list of secret complaints and resentments, and that's a recipe for disaster.

One partner thinks everything is fine, and the other is on her way to divorce. The same phenomenon occurs in dating. Almost all of us are guilty of becoming chameleons when we date. We forget everything that made us successful in other aspects of our lives. Some of us, however, take it to more of an extreme than others.

> **Client:** I'm in debt ... bad. I can't keep up with his lifestyle. My new boyfriend wants me with him all the time at all of his functions. I don't have the clothes for all these fancy functions, so I go out and buy them with money I don't have. I'll never wear these outfits if I'm not with him. Now I have debt on my credit cards. I've never spent money I don't have. I don't know how I'm going to pay off my credit cards. I'm thousands of dollars in debt.

> **Therapist:** How about saying when the next invitation comes, I would love to go, but I don't think I have the clothes necessary for that event. I really enjoy being with you and doing these things with you, but I've been spending money I don't have for other events we've gone to together. Debt is something I have never allowed to happen to me. I've never spent what I don't have. I'm really uncomfortable, and scared actually. I need to change my ways. I hope you understand.

I have had clients who regretted taking too much time off work to travel with men, and others who gave up good jobs without first discussing how money was going to flow into the new marriage.

We can't simply join "his world" willingly without requiring him to do the same of ours. Otherwise, at best, we're left being resentful, and at worst, we're left both resentful and broke.

> **Client:** I go to every one of his boring events, yet he hasn't met a single one of my friends. I spend time with his kids, yet I can feel them hating me, feel them almost calculating how much of their inheritance I'm costing them. Do you realize he won't go to my parents' thirtieth wedding anniversary? My whole family is going to be there. I'm so angry I don't know what to do.

> **Therapist:** How about saying, I'm not going to be able to attend this function or that function with you. Your children have expressed a desire to have some alone time with you, so I will honor that request. I'm really going to miss you at my family's gathering. Everyone's asking about you, and they were all hoping this would be their

opportunity to meet you. I hope you will join me with my family sometime soon.

We have to take care of ourselves, and when things get lopsided, it becomes that much more difficult. To keep things from getting lopsided, we must have a voice in our relationships.

Client: I feel like I'm begging when I ask my husband for money. I can't stand it. I've always made my own money and never had to ask anyone to take care of me.

Therapist: Tell him there's an important and potentially difficult conversation you would like to have, and ask him to pick a time.

Begin by telling him you made a mistake by not having this conversation sooner (bad business decision on your part). Give him a short synopsis of your relationship with money, particularly as it relates to your recent past and your career.

Be open to hearing about his history with women and money. Be clear what you are asking for. If he asks what you would need to be happy, give him an amount. Don't say, "I don't know, what do you think?"

Be clear on what you need in order not to build resentment. Discuss, take a break, discuss. Talk to trusted friends (other adults who may have worked this out, not rabble-rousers).

Keep the discussion going until neither party has resentment, keeping in mind that men are more inclined to try to solve problems than they are to express the empathy and compassion you might receive from your female friends.

Just give him the breakdown, and let him solve it. If it's a different solution than you had in mind, you can either accept it or decline.

Homework

When, and under what circumstances, have you been a chameleon? If doing things "his way" is the only way, then it's time to assess the situation, not ignore it, as that can only lead to further resentment.

If our requests are declined time after time, then at some point, we have to admit to ourselves that we're not really involved in an equitable relationship at all.

Ask yourself what type of relationship you want, not what type of relationship you think you're a good enough person to ever find, or what type of relationship he tells you you're not good enough to find.

While it's important to take care of ourselves in all domains, it's particularly important to take care of ourselves in the domain of finances. It's one thing to heal a broken heart, quite another to heal a broken heart along with a broken wallet.

Resentment kills passion, so it's not uncommon for people-pleasers to have affairs. The people-pleaser feels justified, because, "Look at all the injustices my partner has committed." Wrong!

> **Client:** I have a wonderful man in my life. He's warm, funny, adores me, and listens to me. He cares what I'm doing, how I'm doing, and—you know what?—I deserve him. He's the exact opposite of my husband. What do I do?
>
> **Therapist:** Close one door before you open another. If you want warm and fuzzy, tell your husband. If you still don't get it, require it. Yell, scream, do whatever you need to do to get his attention, but get it. Then drag his cute, cold, little self into therapy, and see if he can deliver what you think you want. Ask! Ask for what you need!

How many people leave their marriage for the next person, only to leave the next person because they did not really know him? How many families have been traumatized because someone had an affair, only to leave the affair?

Close one door before you open another, and make sure you actually hear the door shut behind you.

It is our job in a partnership to have the courage to bring up our concerns, to give our partner the opportunity to address those concerns and fight for the marriage. Ending a marriage in which one person has not had the chance to fight to keep it produces suffering that can take years to get over.

The Children

Then there are the children of the divorced family. The children, of course, no longer have full access to both parents. What if dad forgets about me? What if mom forgets about me? What about new spouses and new children coming on the scene?

Fearing abandonment, what do you think children do, particularly daughters? You guessed it: They take on people-pleasing skills.

Abandonment is a very real concern for children of divorce. Research tells us that those children, especially daughters, are more worried about losing dad, and sometimes, dad uses this fear for manipulative purposes. This can be for a variety of unhealthy reasons, sometimes unconsciously, sometimes not. [19]

> **Client:** My parents are divorced, and my dad lost his job. I think I should cancel my summer plans and go live with him, give him some support, and make sure he's looking for a new job.
>
> **Therapist:** Actually, given that you are eighteen and your dad is forty-five, I think you are both adults, and it is not your responsibility. Dad probably has his network of support, as you do, and he can rely on them.
>
> It's a nice thought, but I don't think it makes sense for you to be the mom, making sure he does what he is supposed to do. It takes an emotionally healthy parent to reassure children during divorce, to provide a stable, predictable, consistent, loving environment for them to move forward in and become autonomous, authentic, young adults. Unfortunately, that is not always the case.
>
> **Client:** I'm worried about going away to college. My mom recently went through a divorce and is alone. I'm the oldest son, and I think I should stay home and help her.
>
> **Therapist:** I'm sorry your mom and your family went through a divorce, but she is not your responsibility. It is in your mom's best interest for you to get back to normal as soon as possible. That means going to the school of your dreams. You can be in closer contact than you might

otherwise have been, but really, what mom needs is to find other people going through what she is going through, and develop her own network of support.

Blame

When divorce breaks up a family, children often blame mom regardless of whether dad was a womanizer, had an affair, or was an absentee dad and husband.

So many fabulous women I've worked with feel that their children, particularly their daughters, blame them for their failed marriages.

It's not just the kids who are likely to feel this way; it's also society in general that tends to feel it's the woman's job to keep the marriage together.

It takes emotionally healthy parents to address this issue responsibly. Otherwise, dysfunctional patterns can and will develop in their children.

In some cases, one parent is "stronger," and "protects" the children from unpleasant aspects of the "weaker" one. In other cases, the parents are stronger as a couple than as two separate individuals.

In either instance, unfortunately, when divorce occurs, the strong part of the parental bond, however it may have manifested itself, usually disappears. The children are left at a time of major crisis to deal with two separate individuals and all their foibles. [20]

People-Pleasing Parents

Of course, if one of the parents is a people-pleaser, the results can be devastating. I've seen it happen before the first child is even born.

Client: All these people are coming to watch the birth. They're expecting to be in the same room with me, and I'm starting to panic. I don't know if I want so many people around, but my husband is putting pressure on me to be nice to everyone. After all, it's everyone's first grandchild.

Therapist: What do you want?

Client: I don't know. He's right. It is everyone's first grandchild, and my husband just wants to please the families. Who am I to take away that experience for the grandparents?

Therapist: You're the child's mother.

Client: Oh!

Therapist: Let's talk first about how you, and then your husband, want to welcome your first child. If you're unhappy with your environment, that will translate to your child. Mom and unborn child are the two most important people to be supported at the time of the birth.

How about saying to your husband, Honey, I'd like us to be alone for the birth of our first child. Everyone can be in the waiting room. I'm just not comfortable with an audience. And then your husband can say to the families, We've decided it will just be the two of us in the delivery room, and once our child is born, the grandparents can rotate in. Thanks for understanding.

Homework

Can you see how people-pleasers cannot properly take care of others? Think back to the story of Julie's mom, too.

People-pleasers think they can take care of the addicts in their lives, and they think they can take care of their children, but what addicts, children, and other dependents need are boundaries and someone who can enforce those boundaries.

Simply put, if we can't take care of ourselves, we can't take care of others.

One of the best examples of what happens to children with people-pleasing moms comes courtesy of the least likely of all places: the crude, Comedy Central cartoon sitcom called South Park.

Cartman is the obese, spoiled, bigoted, heartless brat everyone loves to hate. And his mom is the town slut: Not only is she unable to say No to her son, she also is unable to say No to any man in the whole town of South Park, Colorado.

It's funny, unless Cartman's behavior happens to mimic that of our own children. Children will act out and continue to act out until we stop trying to please them. It isn't our job to give them everything they ask for, which is exactly what Cartman's mom does. Instead, it is our job to love, guide, and discipline with confidence.

Beyond the Family

Moms are not the only people who must learn to say No. The results of people-pleasing extend well beyond the individual and the family. Their impact is seen and felt in communities worldwide.

When schools don't stand up to bullies, for example, the entire student body feels the consequences. Students don't have a safe environment in which to learn, and the victims have lifelong negative consequences.

When U.S. regulatory agencies fail to enforce rules and regulations governing financial institutions, the effects are pervasive. The current economic crisis cost hundreds of thousands of people their jobs and savings, not just here at home but around the world as well.

When churches don't take action against sexually abusive priests, entire belief systems are compromised, and the victims suffer lifelong consequences.

In the world today, it's imperative to have the backbone to say No.

In the northeast community where I worked some time ago, when drug dealers moved into "the projects," all the mothers banded together to report who they were, which led to their being kicked out and/or arrested. This is an example of women banding together and producing a power greater than one. We can all learn from their courage.

The movie Pray the Devil Back to Hell chronicles thousands of women who banded together to end the civil war in Liberia. [21] These were otherwise-ordinary women of all ages who took on warlords in order to restore peace to their war-ravaged homeland. All wore white T-shirts with six simple words on the back: We Want Peace. No More War.

But those few words represented so much of what we're talking about:

- *The ability to say No*

- *The ability to make requests*

- *The ability to speak authentically*

These women risked their lives, reminding us that there are many countries in which women don't have the same rights we do. We have all seen with horror how the Taliban treat women.

"The people who did this to me don't want women to be educated. They want us to be stupid things," reported Shamsia Husseini, one of eleven Afghan girls who returned to class after being attacked with acid two months earlier. [22] Note that this young woman is saying No in a very dangerous situation.

Remember the young Afghan Olympian who said her brother would kill her for competing in the 2000 Summer Games?

The reformist movement in Iran marching and chanting "Death to the Dictator," taking a stand for justice and freedom!

Viewed from this perspective, it's almost our patriotic duty as women to be the independent thinkers and doers that our own laws have evolved to allow us to be. If we don't, what message are we sending the women of Liberia, Afghanistan, and other countries around the world?

It is our worldly duty to speak up. The informant who alerted police to the terrorist plot planned for Heathrow Airport in London had the backbone to say, "No, I don't think so."

And, of course, on September 11, 2001, the forty-four passengers and crew members of Flight 93, armed with nothing more than courage, stood up and said No to the hijacking terrorists.

We can't help but remember with tears Todd Beamer's words, "Let's roll," as they changed destiny by changing the direction of their plane, which crashed in a field just outside Shanksville, Pennsylvania, and not into the terrorists' target.

And Jasper Schuringa, who with the help of others on Northwest Flight 253 stopped Umar Farouk Abdulmutallab from blowing the plane up en route from Amsterdam to Detroit.

Find a hero for yourself. Find someone whose courage to say No gets your juices going! Put this hero on your wall, in your wallet, anywhere and everywhere. Jump on the train of dignity, beginning with the ability to say No to all the toxicity, negativity, and insecurities that stand in the way!

Heard enough?

Ready to learn how to say No?

Me too. Let's get started.

CHAPTER TWO

THE SCIENCE OF SAYING NO

Simple or Not?

On the surface, it appears to be a pretty simple proposition: Just say No!

Sometimes, it is simple:

- *"Want to go for a hike?"*
- *"Should we have the Mansons over for dinner?"*
- *"How about some of Mom's meatloaf?"*

Sometimes, it's not so simple, though—for example, as we negotiate our way through life:

- *"Would you like to go out with me Saturday night?"*
- *"Can I borrow $50? It would really help me out."*
- *"Would you mind watching my kids after school?"*

And sometimes, it's impossible—for example, if you're in an abusive relationship and at risk of injury. But most of the time, it's OK to say No, so let's define exactly what we're talking about.

And as a start, because it's often easier when it comes to Saying No, let's discuss what it's not about:

Saying No Is Not About Providing Excuses

For example, my friend's sixteen-year-old daughter has epilepsy. She loves her time at home with her family, and often doesn't want to go out with friends. At the same time, she doesn't want to hurt her friends' feelings. Her dad's advice to his daughter was to "play the epilepsy card."

"There are plenty of times," he told her, "that epilepsy doesn't work in your favor. You might as well work it to your advantage when you can. Just tell your friends you've been having seizures and aren't feeling up to it."

While dad's advice was well-intentioned, it is detrimental to his daughter. In essence, it's teaching her people-pleasing behavior and habits, specifically:

- *To feel guilty about saying No*
- *That it's bad to have and express true feelings*
- *That something about her isn't normal and is "less than"—as opposed to the idea that there's something about everyone that isn't "normal," that everyone has some "thing" in their life, and that that's what makes us each unique*

If you think about the excuses you use, they almost always make you a victim. Illness is an overused story for not wanting to do something.

> *"I don't feel well."*

> *"I'm tired."*

> *"I didn't sleep well."*

Even if and when any of these are true, there's no reason to mention them. Warriors say No with dignity, not with excuses:

> *"No, I can't do that. Thanks for asking. I hope you'll ask me again."*

Saying No Is Not a Rejection

If I ask you to get me a cup of tea and you say No, your answer can have nothing to do with me or whether you like me. No is not a reflection of your emotions. It is an answer to a question. If we can truly internalize this interpretation, our lives will become so much easier.

I remember a conversation I had with a salesman about the annual renewal of some advertising. When I gave him my final decision to cut my advertising in half for the coming year, he said, "You're doing this because you don't like me!"

At this point, I had known this man for fifteen minutes. I was expanding my advertising into different areas. Those two statements were facts. I made my decision based on diversifying my advertising, not on my like or dislike of this person.

I had a similar experience with a car salesman who refused to allow me to decline. In our conversation about price, he said, "If I ask my manager to go to this low price, you have to accept the offer. I can't ask him if you won't buy the car at this price." I walked out and found a salesman at a different dealership who was free to negotiate until we were both satisfied.

Unfortunately, I believe many of us are trapped in the interpretation that saying No is a rejection. If it hurts me to hear No, it must hurt you, so I will protect all of us. I won't say No to you, and I won't ask questions in a way that you can say No to me.

Where's the dignity in that?

People-pleasers expend a great deal of energy during conversations trying to avoid confrontation. We formulate questions and statements designed to avoid use of the word "No," as opposed to the questions and statements that best express our true feelings.

How can we walk with dignity if we can't speak with integrity? How can we have self-knowledge if we spend more time formulating thoughts, statements, and responses that don't represent our true feelings than those that do?

Saying No Is Not About Controlling Outcomes

When we say No, it doesn't mean we're control freaks. Saying No is simply an expression of what we can or cannot do.

If we don't like the pre-nup, for example, it doesn't mean we're being unreasonable. It simply means there are aspects of it we don't like.

It becomes important, however, that we are able to express what it is we like and dislike. If all we have is the ability or courage to say, "I don't like it," then—even if we don't intend to—we might very well come across sounding like control freaks, even to ourselves.

On the other hand, if we set standards for ourselves and can state clearly why we don't feel they are being met, then it's clear to everyone that we're simply being dignified in our ways, not controlling.

What happens when people sign pre-nups with which they're uncomfortable?

They begin the marriage with resentment, and, slowly but surely, chip away at it like they're felling a redwood with a hand ax.

Homework: Some of us are better at articulating our thoughts than others. If you struggle with words, the best way to improve is the same way you would approach any activity you wanted to do better: Practice.

You can practice in front of the mirror, or you can practice with a partner.

Saying No Does Not Mean We're Difficult

When we say No, it does not mean we're being a pain in the ass. Once again, it is simply an expression of what we can or cannot do.

And what we can or cannot do relates directly to the standards we set for ourselves. It doesn't relate at all to the way we may feel about a person.

But that's one of the worst fears of the people-pleaser: that someone will think we don't like them. So there's this constant paranoia that we're being difficult or a pain in the ass.

Homework

What you call being difficult, I call being differentiated. You need to have opinions and standards for how people can or cannot treat you. [23]

People-pleasers want to fit in and not be noticed. But this keeps you from having an opinion that's different from what you think other people's opinions are.

If it helps you become a little bolder, practice pretending you are in a contest to be the best bitch you can be. People-pleasers don't make good bitches, but we all need at least a little bit of bitch in us that we can store away in reserve for use at the right time.

Stop your addiction to being nice! Find another adjective to aspire to, such as: alive, passionate, colorful, exciting, or unpredictable.

> **Client:** My boyfriend of a year says he's not sure I am the one. He wants to see other women before he closes the deal with me. I'm so afraid I might lose him. I feel that I should go along with his request. What should I do? It breaks my heart to think of him with another woman, but I think I have to do this. I actually think he is bored with me.
>
> **Therapist:** Well, let's get bored off the table. This may be the hardest and best move you have ever taken in the love domain.
>
> The adult men I see in my office tell me they like a woman who requires them to be the best they can be. How about if you say, Great idea, let's shake things up a bit. We will both see other people and not each other. If I'm still available after you've checked out your other options, we can talk. If not, it was nice spending time with you. I know I'm a great mate for someone, and if that someone isn't you, there's no reason to drag this thing out if it's not going anywhere.
>
> **Client:** Wow, I don't think he meant that we wouldn't see each other. I think he wants to have his cake and eat it, too.
>
> **Therapist:** Do you want that?
>
> **Client:** I think that if I agree to it, I'll be so insecure and needy I'll be a drag to date anyway.

Therapist: The right relationship is the one in which you are eager to be the best you can be. You are telling me his offer is going to facilitate your being insecure, needy, and clingy. Is that what you want?

Client: No, I actually feel energized just by the idea of taking a stand for what a great partner I am, and saying No to the B.S. he's trying to sell me on.

Therapist: Ahh, a nice bit of the warrior/bitch lady is being born.

Speak Up!

Here's an ironic twist: a therapist trying to bully his client, who also happened to be my client!

My client was in couple's therapy with his wife. Their therapist was pushing hard for a desired outcome for the couple, and the man had to remind the therapist each week of feelings he'd expressed in previous sessions.

Client: Every week, when my wife and I attend therapy, I feel as though everything I said the week before has been discounted. We begin the session as though we're working on this viable marriage, whereas I explained the week before that they did not have my buy-in to a viable marriage.

Therapist: How about if you begin the session with a recap of what you said previously, then add, Let's start from here.

In a similar situation, another client going through a tough divorce had a lawyer she didn't trust.

Client: Every time I see my lawyer, he tells me what I can't get and how I should go easy on my husband. I don't trust that he's best representing me—my husband, maybe, but not me!

Therapist: Have you told him how you feel?

Client: No, I'm afraid I might upset him, and I need him now.

Therapist: Actually, you need someone you can trust, even if you have to start over entirely. Both parties in a divorce need to be able to negotiate to the point that when all is said and done, each feels he or she has had a chance to fight their best fight. Otherwise, there's resentment.

I recommend you have a conversation with your lawyer about how you feel. If he doesn't do what you need him to do, think long and hard about what next steps you should take that are in your best interest.

Ultimately, the client hired a new lawyer, who she finally felt was "on her team." It was a minor inconvenience but well worth the interruption, and thank goodness she did. Later, we discovered that the first lawyer had been through his own divorce just before taking on my client's case. Objectivity might not have been his strongest suit at the time.

Mind Reading

Client: I'm so angry with my wife that I feel like I don't even like her.

Therapist: Have you told her what's bothering you?

Client: No, it's hard for me, and I think she ought to know anyway. I'd know what I was doing wrong if she was upset.

Therapist: Really? Where did you get your degree in mind reading? I've been in this business of the mind for a long time, and I can't read minds. What makes you think you can?

Client: First, she didn't give me what I wanted for my birthday, and she should know what I want. I could tell you what she wants at any given moment.

She hasn't cooked my favorite meal in weeks. It's linguine with clams, and she used to cook it once a week. She would always leave a love note in my lunch box, and she hasn't done that in a long time. She just isn't taking care of me the way I think she should.

Therapist: What is going on in your wife's life?

Client: Well, we have a new baby, who takes a lot of her time, but she isn't working. I'm carrying us financially.

Therapist: What do you think your wife needs at this time?

Client: Well, she's always wanted a baby, so I think she probably has everything she wants.

Therapist: Well, if you haven't asked her what she needs during such a life-changing event, you just failed Mind Reading 101. Let's try a new way of being in your marriage: You say No to mind reading and Yes to conversations. Speak up.

The Second Time Around

Client: My new wife and I fight about only one thing: She feels I spoil my children from my first marriage. I actually do give them everything they ask for, so she's probably right. But their mom's a drug addict—as in non-functioning drug addict—and when I was younger, I was a workaholic and never around.

Therapist: Do you think your kids know this about you? Let me put it another way: Do you think your kids are working you because they know you feel guilty?

Client: I never thought so, but my new wife absolutely thinks they do.

Therapist: How is this really helping you, or anyone, for that matter?

Client: I feel like I'm there for them now.

Therapist: Did your father give you everything you asked for? Should any parent give any child everything she or he asks for? [24]

Client: Probably not. But I feel so guilty.

Homework

Is this you? Feeling guilty about something accomplishes nothing.

Take responsibility for your actions by having conversations about what you feel so guilty about. Speak up! Ask to have a conversation with all of your children. Bring up the past, and ask each of them how your behavior affected them in their lives.

- *Were you absent most of the time?*

- *Were you high most of the time?*

- *Were you broke? Sad? Short-tempered?*

Tell them: I think I might have been overly consumed with building my business at the expense of you kids and the family. What do you think?

Let each child talk about his or her experience. Listen for blame, pain, sadness, and anger, and discuss everyone's emotions. Allow your children their illusions, their magical thinking, their experience of what happened, apologize for your part, and continue the conversations until the experiences can be filed under "Resolved." Whatever the issue, handle it this way. [25]

If you never do this, you will raise spoiled children. What's more, they will still carry their pain and unresolved issues.

If no one, particularly our parents, ever talked to us directly about real issues, then it's unlikely we will think to do it ourselves. But we must.

If you're afraid that letting your children bring up their issues means they might not like you, you are literally blackmailing yourself, to the point that you will never say No to your children. Everyone loses in that scenario.

Not from a material perspective, of course, but in terms of thoughtless, insensitive, hurtful actions of the past, those things will forever remain unresolved.

You need to be able to say No to anyone and everyone but especially to your children.

You also need to be accountable for your actions with everyone but especially your children.

These breakdowns are more common than you think. Many people refuse to stop spoiling their children, and in so doing, cause substantial damage to their marriages and their children both.

People-Pleasing Symptoms

Are you scared to speak up? When you say No, do you:

- *Accompany it with an excuse?*

- *Feel like you're rejecting someone?*

- *Feel like a control freak?*

- *Feel like you're being difficult?*

- *Feel like you're causing conflict?*

If you do, it's very likely you are engaged in some form of people-pleasing.

And there are other symptoms, too, which are less easy to self-identify without some explanation:

- *Overachievement accompanied by low self-esteem* [26]

- *Adherence to mainstream thinking;*

- *Mistaking drama for excitement.*

People-pleasing is a deep crevasse to climb out of—no question—because the causes are deep-rooted, but we've been through worse, right?

Overachievement Accompanied by Low Self-Esteem

One client who showered and washed her hair for our first session (even though it was over the phone!) had bloody knuckles by the time she made it out of the crevasse.

When she heard her husband pull into the driveway, she would hang up. She hid payment for our sessions from her husband, too. We couldn't meet in person until years later.

The woman had a history of abandonment, loss, and neglect. One parent died when she was young, and the other parent turned to alcohol to deal with the pain. As many children do in these and similar situations, my client stepped up to take care of the surviving parent and raise her siblings.

And as an adult, she did what many adults who have walked in her shoes do. She recreated her history, attracting people in her personal life who delivered abandonment, loss, and neglect. She responded as she had done as a child, by overachieving.

In fact, the worse the situation was, the stronger she felt. She could handle anything! The abandonment, loss, and neglect fed her poor self-esteem and insecurities, while the overachieving fueled her lack of standards for the way people could treat her as well as her arrogance about how much she could handle.

She relished the fact that she was so strong and not a complainer. In her mind, complaining about toxicity and abuse was weak. She was the quintessential, people-pleasing overachiever with little self-esteem.

Client: I'm a bad wife. I have ADD, and don't know how to run a house. There are boxes, piles, and messes everywhere. I can't finish anything. I hoard all my possessions from childhood. My husband's doctor says there's something seriously wrong with me. I have seven children, who seem to be doing really well. I'm not sure how, but they are.

Therapist: Can you see that you alternate from handling more in a day than most of us do in a lifetime to feeling worthless? One minute, you report handling monumental challenges; the next minute, you can't find anything redeeming about yourself, and are inclined to believe anyone who decides to vomit on you. Neither interpretation is right, and you need emotional boundaries.

Client: I know I'm a good person. I have more love and kindness than most people I know. People who really know me say I'm the most beautiful person they know.

Therapist: When you describe how people who love you speak about you, you are closer to where you want to be. You need to develop standards for how you will allow people to treat you, and standards for the sort of environments in which you will allow yourself to be.

It takes strength to require people to respect you. Your definition of strong is, I can handle all the toxic environments I find myself in. That is not strong to me; that is being a victim.

It takes strength to push back against people who want to vomit on you. Real strength is requiring people to respect you and treat you well.

Once you take a stand against the bullshit in your life, the loving person that's inside you will be more authentic. If the loving person is nothing more than a symptom of people-pleasing, it isn't real.

To better understand this concept, rent the movie Pray the Devil Back to Hell. [27] The Liberian women became warriors when they had to. When they disbanded their organization, they disbanded it with powerful words: "We will be back if the fighting comes back. We will be back if our children or country need us to come back." All of us need warrior energy.

Strength is not what you can handle. Survival is what you can handle. Strength is having the courage to say No to toxic people and places.

But it's difficult to recognize and accept how toxic our worlds are. We get caught up in the idea that we are the nice people, and that those who have standards are the difficult ones.

Sometimes, we gain weight, shut down, or become numb rather than feel the pain of the toxicity we have allowed ourselves to believe is acceptable. Do you do any of these things?

The conversation I shared with you is one the client and I had countless times. That said, there were major turning points, and one of the biggest was when she shifted her definition of what strong was. It was then that she climbed on the fast track to functional health. The point where I knew we'd arrived was when she started biting off life as fast as she could: enrolling in school, getting out in the community, commitment to self-care, etc.

When we feel the need to make up for lost time, it's a signal that we're on our way to warriorhood.

Mainstream Thinking

When we fall asleep at the wheel of life, there are consequences: addictions, obesity, illness, and destitution. It's imperative that we question mainstream thinking.

For example, we allow ourselves to be brainwashed by marketing when we eat everything that is pushed on us. French fries, pizza, candy, soft drinks, huge portions—obesity rates keep climbing at alarming rates, and we don't stop to think for ourselves: "Do I want to look the way I will look if I eat this?"

How about asking yourself: "Do I want to pay the doctor bills I will pay to be this unhealthy?" What about your family? If we are going to regain our physical dignity, we need to wake our minds and rouse our souls.

The fact that there are people out there who make fortunes filling us with fat, sugar, and nicotine is the topic for another book, but right now, it is up to us to say No. If we say No to the takers and greedheads, their game is over. On the other hand, if we roll over and say nothing, they win.

"No," says the warrior. "You do not have my best interests at heart. No, you are not going to take advantage of me."

Are you able to say No like a warrior? If not, why not? Are you fearful? Of what? The number one answer I hear to this question is fear of confrontation.

We are adults now. We are in a position to rewrite the rules and to clear out the ghosts of confrontation. Confrontation does not have to include yelling, fear, physical threats, disapproval, or anything else we may associate with it that makes us fearful.

Many of us who were raised with raging or disapproving parents have vowed never to be like them. The problem is that we stuff our anger instead.

And more times than not, if we're stuffing our anger, it comes out in the form of passive-aggressive confrontation. In other words, we stab people in the back in order to avoid speaking our truth to them.

Usually, no one—including us—knows what's happened, because our anger comes out sideways. It doesn't address the real issue, and as a result, that real issue is never resolved and continues to rear its ugly head.

We have to be able to confront the takers. Otherwise, they sabotage our lives. If we can't confront the takers, we can't care for the people who want to love us.

Stop the Drama

Client: I've got a new woman in my life. She's exciting, passionate, athletic, and successful—all the things I've always said I want in a partner. My ex must sense that I'm moving on because she keeps calling with different "stories" about why we should get together.

It's funny how before I met this woman, my ex never called, but now, she calls all the time. She stops by my office and suddenly just wants "to be friends." I don't want to hurt her, and maybe she does just want to be friends, but the timing is suspect.

Therapist: The good news is that your read is probably dead-on. When exes suddenly appear around the time that you're moving on, it's no accident.

Consciously or unconsciously, many people don't want us to move on. They have their own insecurities, which become aggravated when others around them "move on."

It is up to us, and us alone, to say No to the people who want to sabotage our success.

I recommend a call, something like this:

Hi Ex! How are you? I wanted to let you know that I'm in a new relationship, and I'm very excited about getting to know this new person.

Right now just isn't the right time for me to be working on a friendship with you. I appreciate the gesture, and maybe sometime in the future, when we're both happy and solid in new relationships, we can see if the four of us might want to have dinner together. Thanks for understanding and respecting my wishes.

It is always amazing, even to me, how many people do not want to put healthy closures on past relationships. Sometimes, I guess, we want to keep someone "in the wings," just in case the new relationship doesn't work out. But there is a difference between an ex who is now a friend and an ex who is now a hanger-on.

Say No to safety nets and hangers-on.

Drama and Abuse

More times than not, people hang on to past relationships, particularly bad ones, because dysfunctional relationships involve more drama.

Unfortunately, people who have spent a lot of time in dysfunctional relationships can become addicted to the drama. They actually start to think that a healthy relationship or a healthy partner is boring ... ho hum!

But that's backwards. Our relationships should not be full of drama. Life comes with enough excitement and challenges. Instead, our relationships should support us and protect us through the drama that makes up the rest of our lives.

I have seen caring people take daring action to rescue someone from an abusive situation, only to find that the rescued person became angry with the people who "helped" her or him. Lawyers see it all the time when the abuse victim refuses to testify. [28]

It is important for people coming out of an abusive situation to get help immediately. I recommend ongoing individual therapy, group therapy for abuse victims, and/or going away for several days to an intensive workshop dedicated to understanding what happens when we live with abuse and how to move forward from the abuse. Otherwise, we give in to feelings of grief, such as, "I think about it. I miss it. I should be back there." No, these are the same feelings that accompany any loss. They are not a sign that you should return to the situation.

Once we get over this, however, and discover what life has in store for us outside the domain of abuse, the difference between an exciting life and a life filled with drama becomes crystal clear.

When we live with abuse, it becomes our focal point: how much, when it will happen, how we can avoid it, maybe we're bad, maybe we're not, maybe we cause it, maybe we don't.

Remember, the abuser can be either male or female. Both can be equally clever at keeping you in the web. And remember, too: There are organizations whose only purpose is to protect you and help you out of an abusive relationship.

For homework, ask yourself this: Is it exciting? Interesting? And answer yourself honestly: Is it interesting to your friends to hear about it?

Step One is getting out. If the abuser can get the victim out of therapy, odds are better that the victim will stay trapped.

Step Two is staying out. While it will feel like a gigantic magnet pulling you back, you have to resist. You might miss the intensity most of all. "This is so boring," you'll tell yourself. "It may be healthy, but it sure is boring."

Step Three is to reinvent yourself—quickly. Find a new job, or if you like the one you have now, immerse yourself in it. Travel. Take on a hobby. Whatever it is, find a passion, because, if the abuser can find you, she will.

And when she does, you will want to go with her, because it feels good to be pursued. But as soon as you regain your self-esteem, get a renewed interest in a healthy life, are not attracted to drama any longer, and time passes, you will find your ex's advances irritating. She will become a nuisance. Just the idea of having more of her dramatic bullshit in your life will be enough to set you off.

Leave me alone, you will scream, and you will wonder how you ever put up with the abuse.

Set standards for yourself. As soon as you do, it will no longer feel good to be pursued. It will feel more like Fatal Attraction—someone is trying to intimidate you, threaten you, interfere and subvert you.

"No, I do not want to be with you. Thank you for asking."

Of course, while it is illegal in this country to physically abuse one's children or spouse, many people still have the notion that wives and children are the property of the head of the household. They also believe they can treat their "property" as they may have done in a different country. [29]

Often, all it takes is for two worlds to meet—the world of abuse and the world of talking—for the tide to begin to turn, as it did for this sixteen-year-old boy who landed in the hospital.

> **Client:** I know the nurses called you to come talk to me because they heard my dad yelling that he was going to beat me when I got home. I know you are a nice lady who only wants to help, but let me tell you, I am from a very close family that takes care of itself. We don't want help from "the system." My dad's dad hit him, my dad hits me, and that's just the way it is.
>
> You're not going to change him. He doesn't even speak English very well.
>
> **Therapist:** Unfortunately, in this country, if your dad hits you, there are consequences. Maybe we can all meet and talk things out so he doesn't have to resort to hitting. You be the translator; make sure he understands everything I say.
>
> **Client:** Okay; but I am not optimistic.
>
> **Therapist:** I am!

The meeting took place in the hospital, with family, therapist, and nurses waiting anxiously outside the room.

Dad was a fisherman, an extremely honorable profession in his town and culture, and one where sons followed their fathers, making it a family profession. Dad had a new fishing boat and was taking it out for the first time. His son—left at home, not wanting to go to school, wanting to work by dad's side on the new fishing boat—had a party because he knew mom would call dad to come in to get things under control.

The boy was, in fact, acting out because he wanted to be on the boat with dad. In the hospital session, after dad had yelled at his son for the party, the son was able to tearfully tell his dad what he really wanted. Dad, in tears, tried to explain that he wanted his son to finish school before he started fishing, but secretly was honored that his son wanted to be with him.

The meeting was the first to show this family that talking is more powerful than hitting. It was very emotional for all of us.

> **Client:** I saw you crying. My dad likes you for a "system lady."
>
> **Therapist:** Thanks. Tears and talking are good.

How Did We Get Here?

You may ask yourself, "Well, how did I get here?"

—*Talking Heads* [30]

What happens in our lives that we develop this inability to say No? This desire to avoid confrontation at all costs? It's not as if we're born with it. Babies, for example, have no problem sealing their lips, turning their heads, and pushing spoonsful of food away.

When we're raised in an environment in which parenting is compromised or essentially nonexistent, it is common for the child to become the parent.

We become competent in areas we wouldn't and shouldn't be. We stand on chairs to reach the cupboards for food for our siblings and ourselves. We stay at home to watch over our drunken dad and clean the house, instead of playing with the other eight-year-olds.

We lie about why we want to stay home, why we don't want our friends (if we still have any left) to come over, and why we always walk or bike to school, instead of being dropped off like all the other kids.

We pretend we're not hurt when dad Indian burns us to exert abusive power, and pretend we're not scared when mom drives us drunk. We pretend we can drive at an early age because we think we are a better driver sober at age ten than mom is drunk at age forty.

These become our standards. We don't say No because we can't say No. If we do, we think we will perish, one way or another.

Instead, we become overachievers: cleaning the house, feeding the children, enduring pain, driving. We develop a tolerance for toxic behavior.

Often, things are so intense, and there's so much to do that we don't even know that what is happening in our house is not the norm in other houses.

To what extent are we, as children, willing to go to help our family?

I consulted to a sixteen-year-old girl who was admitted to the hospital because she was cutting her wrists, but she wasn't suicidal.

What she wanted was to get into the "system," in the hope that the system would be able to help her dad who was drinking himself to death. (Dad had an incurable disease that he was treating with alcohol. He would tell anyone who wanted him to stop drinking that he wanted to die rather than stay alive with this disease.)

The girl told me that her dad would come home drunk at 2 a.m. with sub sandwiches for them. He would wake her so they could eat their sandwiches, talk, and be together. Mom apparently had declined the sub sandwich gathering.

> **Client:** I'm often tired at school because I have to get up at 2 a.m. when my dad comes home from the bars with sub sandwiches and I don't want him to eat alone.
>
> **Therapist:** Do you know that other sixteen-year-olds are not eating sub sandwiches with their dads at two in the morning?
>
> **Client:** I didn't, but I think you may be right.

Dad had the right idea in wanting to spend time with his daughter, because he was checking out. But both the time and the conversations themselves (drunken) were inappropriate. I told him that if he was going to keep drinking in order to die, he had to get up every morning early and sober to be with his daughter. He had to answer all the questions she might have of him:

- *Who is going to walk me down the aisle when I get married?*

- *What type of a man should I marry?*

- *Should I go to college or right into my profession? (She was a superb dancer.)*

- *What should I do if my husband drinks too much?*

- *How can I take care of mom and still pursue my dancing?*

Dad actually stopped drinking for some time after being given this assignment to do sober.

If we were raised with abuse, addictions, or dysfunction, it may not have been safe to say No.

> **Client #1:** My husband is a good man. But when he drinks too much, it's a little difficult for all of us in the house. Last week, he came home drunk and threw the two older girls' beds out the window because their bedspreads were crooked. He's pretty strict, and when he's drunk, it's worse.
>
> **Therapist:** Does he hit your children?
>
> **Client #1:** No, just me. He doesn't hit me if my little one is in the room. She rarely leaves my side. I don't think she knows why she stays by me, do you, honey?
>
> **Client #2:** No. I like to be with my mommy.
>
> **Therapist:** Protecting you is a big burden for a six-year-old, Mom. Are you drinking as well?
>
> **Client #1:** Yes, it helps me deal with the situation.
>
> **Therapist:** It may feel like it helps you deal with it, but drinking actually makes it worse.
>
> **Client #1:** I think you may be right. I'm here in your office for the first time because I think you may be right. I need to make my home safe for all of us.
>
> **Therapist:** This may be your toughest and most rewarding journey. You don't have to live with this abuse. With sobriety and recovery, you and your family can

regain your dignity, live in a safe home, and live your lives. If your husband wants to join you in a sober, dignified, recovering home, he will have to abide by the new standards. Beds will not be flying out the window, and six-year-olds will not be security officers.

The first step, of course, is to remove ourselves from a situation in which it is physically unsafe to say No. Once we're out of that sort of situation, it is time for us to begin to learn how to say No.

As we progress, there are four signs we can use to monitor our progress. They tell us if we're saying Yes when we should be saying No:

- *Resentment*

- *Anger when others make requests of us: (You want what?)*

- *Out-of-character blowups*

- *Avoiding relationships*

Resentment

Resentment is "you owe me." If we make an agreement, money for a car, and I give you the car but your check bounces, I am going to build resentment if I don't take action to have you fulfill your part of the agreement. This is an easy one. If, however, I "make up" that you owe me—e.g., my parents should have been model parents; or I paid last time, so you should pay this time; or I'm nice, so you should be nice to me; and on and on—then I will also have resentment based on ideas I made up.

Resentment is a feeling with which we want to become intimate. It provides instant feedback, and therefore is a very valuable tool. Embrace it, and it will help you start taking care of yourself.

Sometimes, we think we're capable of saying No when, in fact, we're not. Any time we find ourselves harboring feelings of resentment, there's a good chance we've been saying Yes when we should have been saying No.

Client: I am always paying for things. If I go to lunch with my friends, I always pay, and they never reciprocate. Same with my husband.

I see to all his needs. I do nice things for him every day. He never does anything nice for me. He doesn't even thank me. At this point, it's like he expects it—just like the people I go to lunch with. People take me for granted.

Therapist: Are you asked to pay or do you offer? Does your husband ask you to do those things, or do you just do them?

Client: I just do them, because I think it's the nice thing to do. No one asks me. I keep thinking someone else will pick up the bill the next time, but they never do. I keep thinking my husband will think of me, but he doesn't.

Therapist: Do you think you are guilty of this crazy thing we women do? We give and give and give, build resentment, and then we give some more.

Client: Ick! That sounds just like me.

Therapist: You're not alone. How about if we try life a different way? There's nothing wrong with giving, so how about if you give only to the point where you have absolutely no expectations that anyone will give back to you?

In other words, give only to the point where you can do so without resentment. When you start to feel resentment, you have to stop giving.

For example, the next time the bill comes, define your terms, set your standards: I'll get this one, you get the next. And when that time comes, it won't be such a surprise when you say: I think this is yours; I got it last time.

If you're uncomfortable with that, it's OK. You could also say, Let's split it, then work your way up to a point where you're comfortable saying, I think this one is yours. I got it last time.

You Want What?!

If we feel anger when others make requests of us, it's another sign that we're probably having difficulty saying No. Like resentment, if we pay attention to anger, we can learn a lot about ourselves.

Client: I hate being around her. She is so pushy. Every time I'm with her, she gets me to volunteer for something I don't have time to do. I'm not going to the luncheon because she will be there.

Therapist: No one can get you to do things you don't want to do, except you. Have you ever said No to her?

Client: No, because I feel like I'm a bad person if I don't help out, particularly a charity. What would people say? I don't care. Actually, that's not true. I care too much.

Therapist: Being able to say No to things you don't have time for has nothing to do with the charity. It's about knowing your schedule, your commitments, your priorities, and what you have time for.

Client: What do I say?

Therapist: Thanks for asking, Ms. Pushy. I can't help this time around. Please try me in the future.

Client: Are you kidding? If I can tell her No once, I'm not going to invite her to ask me again. You must be nuts.

Therapist: Probably. But it's good practice. Welcome other people's requests, too, anybody's. Think of them as target practice. If you can respond with a No, it's the equivalent of a bulls-eye.

Blow-Ups

If we blow up from time to time, it's often because we feel as if we haven't done anything for ourselves, only for others. It's important not to dismiss our anger but to instead give its source some thought. It might have a message for us: that we've been saying Yes when we should have been saying No.

We might end up in a fight with our wife about why she hasn't done the laundry. At first, we might think we're pissed about not having any clean shirts, whereas the truth is that we're probably stressed from the money the business is losing, the unhappy customers we talk to regularly, and the long hours we are working.

> **Client:** I'm running a short temper these days. Everyone seems to notice: my kids, co-workers, and my wife! My kids even brought me my meditation shawl the other day—I had just gone off on them. I think it's because I'm stressed out and not taking care of myself. I'm not working out. I haven't meditated in months.

> **Therapist:** OK, let's make a schedule that's designed to succeed. What's the minimum you will do, no matter what—work out, meditate? Let's start with manageable goals. That way, you're more likely to increase the minimum every week. [31]

It is important for you to stop absorbing the stress of life. Push back. I can't talk to you today. How about tomorrow at two? I'll be in late tomorrow. Here's what you have to do to open the business. No, we can't spend money on that; we have to cut back for the next couple of months until the business is more solvent.

For homework, think about what arrangements you can make so you can say No to someone else in order to say Yes to yourself. All of us need to say Yes to ourselves.

Where's Waldo?

People-pleasers often disappear rather than have an honest conversation, which may include saying No to someone.

> **Client:** I was dating this great woman. I loved being with her, and I loved who I was when I was with her. You know what I mean?

> We were together six months. Then because my friends thought I should be with someone else, I just didn't call her one day. Now it's been over a month. I miss her, and I don't know what to do. At first, I thought my friends were right, but now, I don't know.

Therapist: Well, you have two issues: You need to think for yourself, and you need to be able to have authentic conversations.

Client: I didn't want to hurt her, and I didn't know what to do, so I did nothing.

Therapist: Doing nothing hurts more than having an authentic conversation.

Client: What do I do now?

Therapist: Friends can sometimes help us see a toxic situation we might not have seen otherwise. Unfortunately, friends can also be self-serving and not want their friendship with you altered. They don't want to lose their wingman. You have to sort out what you think your friends are doing.

From the relationship you're describing, I think their recommendation might not have been in your best interest. So your first conversation is to tell your friends, Thanks for sharing, and I'll take it from here.

After that, call this woman and tell her the truth. Tell her what happened and what you've done about what happened, and invite her back into your life. If she is available, and feels you can make it safe for her, she might give it another shot. If not, you will have at least cleaned up the mess you made.

Many people have lots of messes that have never been cleaned up because they choose to do nothing vs. having an authentic conversation.

Homework

Think about how you were raised. Were you taught what most girls were: to always be nice, always do what others want, and always say yes? Or were you raised to speak up?

Raising the Stakes on Raising Our Daughters

The new message for women is that relationships are partnerships: You do have a vote. Your opinion matters. Be a partner.

What message are we sending to our daughters? Do they see us living day-to-day in a partnership? If not, how are they going to be anything but compliant when they start to interact with the opposite sex or chat on the Internet (with or without your permission)?

If a young woman has seen her mother allowing abuse, it may be hard for her to set her own boundaries. Sometimes, these young women "coach" their moms to be tougher with their abusive dads but unknowingly allow abuse in other areas of their lives: from teachers, coaches, their brothers' friends.

Sometimes, women give up good jobs to move where their boyfriend wants to live, only to have the relationship go south: The boyfriend has a new girlfriend, and she has no job. Be smart and take care of your finances.

Women aren't necessarily taught to have difficult financial conversations: "Men handle that." Well, in the world today, women work and women need to become comfortable having conversations about money.

If you are complaining about a financial arrangement you've made with someone, it's up to you to know the number it would take to have you not complain. Don't say, "What do you think I should want?" which is a classic people-pleasing comment.

Just thinking about having financial conversations may make you feel sick. Well, think about how sick you're going to feel with an empty wallet. Learning to have financial conversations just takes practice. The first one is awkward, but the two thousandth one is like slicing warm butter.

When we lie to ourselves, it will eventually show up in our bodies. Put another way, our emotional selves will always be reflected in our physical selves.

The Posture of People-Pleasing

I know a woman who was in an abusive relationship for seven years. When she finally got out, a large tumor was discovered in her throat.

Thank goodness it wasn't malignant, but she was lucky. She swears the tumor manifested itself in her throat because that's where her stress was: S*he couldn't speak her emotional truth.*

Our emotions are present in our posture, which is different when we're speaking authentically from when we're not, such as when we're saying Yes when we mean No.

When we are in the posture of any form of people-pleasing, our body follows our mind in searching for the right thing to say. If we separate ourselves from our emotional truth, we're not grounded. How can we be?

"What does this person need from me?"

"How can I get this person to like me?"

"How can I take care of this person?"

"How can I avoid conflict?"

Another set of conversations the people-pleaser is usually having with herself are:

"How can I fit in here?"

"I don't want anyone to see me."

"I'm not worthy of having a different opinion."

"I don't want to rock the boat. I have to be nice."

Many people-pleasers have explained to me that they get caught up in a vicious cycle of putting themselves down, which is why they need to please others. They are afraid that if they speak up, the other person will come back with attacks on their behavior:

"Well, you didn't clean the house."

"You need to get your affairs in order."

"You don't exercise. You're overweight."

"Your family is crazy."

"You didn't finish school."

"You don't even have a job."

Whatever the people-pleasers' insecurities are, they are afraid those insecurities will be used against them if they stand up for themselves. They tell themselves they do not have the right to an opinion or to say No until they fix their own problems.

Do we have to be perfect in order to have an opinion and to say No?

Of course not.

We use the same reasoning to put off change. All our affairs don't have to be in order before we begin taking care of ourselves—before we begin learning, for example, how to say No.

One client used her inability to afford our session fees as the reason she couldn't immediately begin the process of learning to say No.

In contrast, a different client told me fees were no problem, since she now had money she hadn't counted on before. As a result of our

sessions, she was developing the ability to say No in situations that previously had been costing her financially.

Do we ease into it, or go cold turkey?

It's your choice, really.

I worked with one client who found it easier to ease into saying No. In this case, it was a man, and he took the first step of saying, "I don't know" to requests.

Then, when he would arrive home, away from the person he felt he had to please, he was able to ask himself, "Do you want to do this?" The answer was usually No. He was then able to go back and say No. This little tip of "I don't know" opened up a whole new world of being able to take care of himself.

For others of us, it's easier to counter with a different suggestion. For example, "I'll bring you a cup of tea in five minutes." It's important not to over-emotionalize everything. A Yes or No is just that, an answer. Yes, I can. No, I can't. Or No, but I can do this other thing.

Trust your intuition, and don't idolize professionals! Remember the TV ad? I know a man who had a medical condition for two years during which two physicians recommended major surgery, but he declined.

Finally, he visited the teacher of both doctors, only to be told, "No way, you don't need surgery. Take this pill." He did, and the condition cleared up in three days. Trust your authentic, intuitive self.

And trust your physical self, too.

If you assume a strong physical posture, it can help provide the backbone, both literally and figuratively, that you will need to speak authentically.

You want your feet to be firmly planted on the ground with your legs strong and your core at its optimal strength in order to face life with courage and confidence. Hold your shoulders back, keep your head high, and have your voice ring clear and strong.

"No, thank you for asking."

You can practice in front of the mirror. First, have the conversation: "Yes sir, no sir, how high sir," and watch your posture. Notice the physical posture of you abandoning you!

Then assume a posture of strength and have the conversation, "No, thank you for asking. These days, I am honoring myself and my concerns."

You might find it more your style to work with a friend. Working in front of a mirror, go back and forth for at least thirty minutes.

First, have your friend make requests of you to which you respond with Yes's and No's, noticing your body's posture when you say Yes, then No. Make sure you are not offering stories, reasons, or excuses when you say No.

Then make requests of your friend to which he or she also responds both ways. Start with easy scenarios and move to real-life situations.

Work toward scenarios of sex and money. These are where many people have the hardest time.

Eventually, you may want to journal your reactions. What was the physical posture, and what emotions accompanied it? I have had people report wobbly knees, upset stomach, unresponsive voice, crying, etc.

Breathing, music, exercise, and meditation are all ways to move through the physical reactions. [32] It's always important to sort out our physical reactions from our chatter. The chatter is just that: chatter. "You are not good enough. That's being selfish. You're a bad person if you say No. What would your mother say? Don't rock the boat. Don't upset anyone."

We can thank the voices for sharing, but in the end, we need to decline to listen to them. Our physical reactions can be lessened or alleviated with exercises or movements. For example, deep breathing can quiet things down. Music and dancing can get us out of low-key anxiety.

Exercise can tire us out. And long-time meditators know they can quiet the body and the mind with serious practice.

You might want to take it in stages. It's almost always easier to reach a goal when it's broken down into smaller ones.

Goal One: I will be more aware of how, when, and where I take care of others at my own expense, when I say Yes when I really mean No.

Goal Two: I will identify my concerns, beliefs, wants, and needs, and say No to things that don't support me.

Goal Three: I will develop standards for how I allow myself to be treated. I will say No to anything that does not meet those standards.

Goal Four: Each week, I will find an opportunity to stop taking care of someone else at my own expense. Each week, I will say No at least twenty times (or you fill in the number).

Goal Five: I will always, every minute of every day, take a stand for my beliefs, my concerns, and me. I will represent only myself, not everyone else in the world. I will learn to say No as easily as I say Yes.

Developing our authentic self is like learning a forehand in tennis. Our first forehand is different from our two thousandth forehand,

and each forehand between one and two thousand has a life of its own.

Some of them, we'll hit too hard, and the ball will fly out of the court. Others, we will mishit, and some we'll miss entirely.

Sometimes, when people begin saying No, they are more forceful, maybe because they're not sure it will work. Other people might be too quiet: "What did you say?" "I said No!" Just keep practicing. The goal is to develop an inner knowing, an awareness, of what is going on with all of our interactions.

Ultimately, we develop the ability to know when and what to say. We find the courage to actually speak authentically. We may even develop the ability to have real silence based on our truth, not on our inability to speak.

All this may seem like a very involved process. Who wants to engage in all that thinking, expend that sort of energy just to have a conversation? The fact is, we already are.

Remember the people-pleasing process?

- *We suppress our own ideas, which we may not even know after so many years of suppressing them.*

- *We attempt to read the mind of the person we're talking to.*

- *We fabricate and articulate an idea that will lead to our being liked and avoid confrontation.*

- *And, as if that isn't enough, this process leads to our expending further energy in the forms of:*

- *Judgmentalism;*

- *Resentment; and*

- *Anxiety.*

That's more than a full, five-set match worthy of the energy expended, and it's all negative. We're going to expend energy as we learn to say No, but at least, it's energy in a positive direction.

With time, the thought process will become unnecessary, and we will work by instinct, the same way experienced tennis players do.

We will have confidence in our ability to take care of ourselves in the domain of No. "Thank you for asking, but I can't do what you've asked."

And then we will see all kinds of things begin to change.

For one, we will attract a different kind of partner. Being empowered to be who we truly are is very seductive to other emotionally strong people. Conversely, not having a sense of self can be a magnet for those who need to control, abuse, or take advantage of others.

Sex and No

We will enjoy sex more. So many women I interviewed said they said Yes to sex when they really just wanted the sex to be over and the person to go away.

Think about this phenomenon for a minute. Your body is very special. It is your body. No one should be allowed to touch it without your permission, and deep down, we all know this.

Conversely, imagine what it's like to want someone to touch your body. What a tremendous pleasure!

> **Client:** I have definitely used sex to get people to like me. I have had sex because I was afraid to say No. How many times have I had sex just to get the person to go away? Countless. I even gained weight so I wouldn't be attractive to people.

> **Therapist:** Do you understand that no one has the right to touch your body without your permission? Do you understand that No means, "No, thank you. I don't want you to touch me right now?" Do you understand that you are worth learning how to say No to unwanted advances? Do you understand that not learning how to say No puts you at risk in the universe? Gaining weight you don't want as a means of saying No is you abandoning you! Stop! Learn how to say No!

As you learn what is important to you in the world, life slows down and becomes easier. You don't have to try all those beauty creams, because you know the one that really supports your skin.

You don't go through the buffet line, because you know what you want to order off the menu.

You don't have all those people around, as they were only there because you were so accommodating. Instead, your friends supports you for who you are and not for who they want you to be.

You have trusted friends who know that you want to hear only the truth from them, because you welcome honest feedback. And they welcome the same from you.

Life gets easier and more enjoyable. As a matter of fact, the anxiety juice that used to come when you were afraid of rocking the boat or being a "pain in the ass" is replaced by warrior juice that makes you a more passionate, alive, and sought-after person.

CHAPTER THREE

MAKING THOSE REQUESTS

Making Requests

For the people-pleaser, the act of making a simple request can be as difficult as asking the hijackers of Flight 93 to please reconsider.

Countless clients I've worked with have somehow made it through the vast majority of their lives without making requests.

Some of us feel as if we shouldn't have to make requests, particularly of those with whom we're close. "If I have to ask," we tell ourselves, "it takes away from the experience." Wrong!

No one is a mind reader, and if we believe that people should know what we need, we will suffer endless disappointment and, ultimately, resentment.

That's why so many of us feel resentment toward our bosses. Typically, the issue is money—specifically, we don't feel we're being paid what we deserve. But do we request more? No. Never.

Other times, wives are resentful of their husbands, and money is often the core issue. "Have you asked your husband for more?" "Oh no, I couldn't do that."

Patterns like this are deep-seated. The roots are planted in childhood.

For instance, I remember my first visit from a divorced mother seeking to improve her daughter's visits with her father. When I asked what would happen if the daughter asked to do activities she enjoyed, she responded: "If she ever made a request, he would hit her."

Hitting a child because she made a request trains the child not to request. Now, look closely with me here. Children are smart, and so—without knowing what or why—this particular girl, seven years old, had learned not to make requests.

Now, fast forward to this girl as a young adult. She will feel tremendous resentment. (Already, at seven, she didn't like visiting dad.) She wouldn't know what she didn't know. She would have no idea that she is not making requests, and no idea that by doing so, she could help end her suffering and unhappiness. Until she put herself in front of a wise therapist, she might not know what was broken and how to fix it. This not knowing is a blind spot that will interfere with her emotional development until the blind spot is revealed to her. [33]

Remember the little girl who shadowed her mother whenever her father was present, subconsciously protecting her mother?

She didn't know she was protecting her mom from being hit by doing that, but she knew something, because she never left mom alone in her dad's presence when she was awake.

Children are wise, adaptable little beings who often take care of the family at the expense of their own emotional health. How does she protect people when she's a young adult? Again, this will be a blind spot for her, needing to be revealed for her emotional health.

There are countless examples of children "keeping" their mom in their own bedroom so she doesn't have to go back to her bedroom with dad.

There are examples of children "unwilling" to leave the master bedroom because of some dysfunction they feel they are addressing by their presence.

How about the little girl who had to stand on the stool to reach the food in the cabinets in order to feed herself and her siblings? She has been trained to take care of herself and others.

Or the girl whose parents purposely denied her requests? She learned that people would hurt you if you gave them the secret information about what is important to you.

Do you think these children grew up feeling comfortable making requests?

Or did they grow up with a tolerance for toxicity?

We are nothing if not creatures of adaptation. We work out, and our muscles adapt to the new stresses placed on them. We study, and our brains adapt to the new stimuli. These adaptations all have the potential to become blind spots.

In children, the process occurs even more readily. Ever notice how much longer it takes to lose ten pounds as an adult than it did as a child?

The process is similar emotionally. We adapt to our surroundings in a way best suited to our survival. If as children, we adapted to take care of ourselves and others at the expense of our own emotional well-being, then that is exactly how we will take care of our family when we become adults ourselves.

Blended Families

Take blended families, for example, those in which the children of divorced parents are absorbed—or, more significantly, sometimes not absorbed—into a new family with new siblings and new stepparents. [34]

How likely is it that these children are going to feel comfortable making requests? What challenges do they face? Even after they become adults, the challenges faced by children of blended families can be almost insurmountable.

One example is the story of Tim McGraw discovering that his real dad was Tug McGraw, the legendary pitcher for the New York Mets and Philadelphia Phillies. [35]

Tim's mom had conceived him out of wedlock, and, as the story goes, when Tim finally met Tug, his dad basically told Tim he wanted nothing to do with him.

By not responding to Tim's phone calls and letters, which amounted to requests for acknowledgment and a father-son relationship, Tug was, in essence, saying, "Let's pretend that night never happened." Well, it probably comes as no surprise to you that I don't support this lesson.

The fact is, if we are the parent of a child, we are the parent of a child. We may choose to have someone else raise that child, e.g., adoption, and that is a responsible alternative to parenting yourself. But it's still our responsibility to see that process through.

Specifically, when we create a child with another person, it is our responsibility to acknowledge the child and see to it that the child is raised in a home in which it is safe to make requests, as well as to say No and to speak authentically.

It is not the child's fault that he was created by his parents. The child did not create himself. If we want to pretend otherwise, that is our burden to bear, not the child's. The child is innocent.

Instead, Tug's behavior sends the message that people need not take responsibility for their actions.

> **Client:** My stepfather has a new girlfriend since divorcing my mom, and we haven't seen him since she came on the scene. He hasn't called and hasn't acknowledged his grandsons' birthdays or any of the holidays. I'm hurt, and I'm upset.

> **Therapist:** Let's talk about what you see as your options and, conversely, what you have to lose.

> **Client:** I want to send a strong letter asking him to get back to being the boys' grandfather, at the very least. I would also like to be part of his life with his new girlfriend, and that will take time.

> He may say No, but I don't think I have anything to lose, since he's not in my life now anyway.

> **Therapist:** OK, let's go over the letter.

Clearly, this client had done her emotional homework. She knew that if her stepfather declined, it was his issue, not hers.

Remember, we can only make the request. We cannot control its outcome.

But we must make that request. Otherwise, we just build up resentment, which is exactly what this client would have done had she not written the letter.

This story had a happy ending. The stepfather actually felt honored that his stepdaughter cared enough to make the request and that she was willing to risk his saying No.

But stories that don't have such a happy ending are far more common.

> **Client:** My dad has remarried and wants nothing to do with his first family. My mom and dad had three children, and he is pretending we don't exist. We think his new wife, who has three children of her own, is pressuring him to disown us and disinherit us, and that he doesn't have the balls to stand up to her.
>
> **Therapist:** Do you understand what a serious betrayal of your family this is by your father?
>
> **Client:** Yes. I think it's why I have such a hard time with men, and why I pick the damaged men I do. None of them are there for me.
>
> **Therapist:** Bingo!

The client, a very successful young woman, eventually paid her dad a visit and asked that he be her father and include her in his life.

He declined and told her to forget he was her dad.

> **Therapist:** What did you say to that?
>
> **Client:** Something along the lines of the oral sex better be pretty hot to be replacing three kids.

Personally, I thought it was more about the father lacking balls, but....

When a parent abdicates responsibility so egregiously, I can applaud such an edgy comment as the one this client made. It shows backbone and helps her stand in a place of knowing that she is not responsible in any way for his abandonment and betrayal.

Given that the divorce rate keeps rising, we can only unfortunately assume that there will be more and more of this type of betrayal. I really encourage children in this situation to take a stand for the truth:

"You are my dad, and I am your daughter/son, and anything you make up to the contrary is just that: something you made up. I will not enable this behavior on your part."

At any time in one's life, the damage done by having a parent forget his financial loyalty and commitments to his original family is challenging. Here are a few examples:

> **Client:** My dad had an affair, ultimately married her, and bailed on all the financial promises he'd made to his children—college, in particular—because his new wife has a different philosophy. (Children should be on their own at age eighteen.) Not only did he promise us a college education but he also spent years insisting that our job was to get into the best college we could, and that his job was to pay for it.

> We are ready to go to college now and have kept our part of the bargain, but dad's financial support is nowhere to be found.

> **Client:** My dad remarried late in life and changed his will so that his new wife received everything. After that, her children got everything. He stopped the traditional Christmas-time checks and any and all financial support we used to count on him for. He was afraid of being alone, so he agreed to all her demands. When he finally did become ill and couldn't mentally care for himself, his new wife asked us, not her own children, for money to care for him!

> Fortunately, we had the presence of mind to say No. We counter-offered to take care of him ourselves, which she declined. When he died, his will confirmed that he had more than enough money to provide for his health care. She just wanted more money for herself.

> Client: My mom remarried, and her new husband thought I looked too much like mom's first husband, my dad. He felt threatened, and told my mom to abandon me. She did!

Homework

The scenarios go on and on, but if you feel like you're getting the short end of the stick, as painful as it is, it's worth it to make the request of your parents that they take responsibility for having created you and keep their agreements.

A good conversation would be any conversation that addresses the new situation. Many blended families do not deal with how things are going to be different and what everyone's input is. Such a conversation might include what the new situation looks like for both parties. What agreements have we had that we might have forgotten? What do we need to speak about going forward?

It doesn't matter what the response is, since you will be maintaining or creating your dignity with the knowledge that you took a stand for yourself. And you must remember: If any parent refuses to take responsibility for creating you, it is about his or her deficiencies, not yours.

Parental Alienation Syndrome

As if all this were not enough, there is another damaging phenomenon called parental alienation syndrome that is also a byproduct of divorce. [36]

What happens is that one parent, subtly or not so subtly, turns a child against the other parent through lies and brainwashing.

If you feel this may have happened, or might be happening to you, do your research. If you have unreasonable, judgmental anger toward one parent, ask yourself why.

Generally, around the age of eighteen, children begin to feel powerful enough (or at least less vulnerable enough) to start scouting around for the truth about their parents and the divorce. Don't believe one angry parent's stories about the other parent. Find out for yourself.

Ask questions. I know one man whose ex-wife spent her whole life turning the children against their father. The father spent years and lots of money fighting her in court, and the kids wouldn't speak to him.

Finally, he'd had enough, and let it go. When each child turned eighteen, he turned over all the court records to them so they could do their own research. He now has a relationship with his children, and they won't speak to their mother. Do your own research. Parents should not use their children for their own insecure, self-serving purposes.

The ability to make requests is critical to ending people-pleasing, living authentically, and walking with dignity.

We must not only be able to make requests of our family members but we also must be able to make requests in every facet of our lives.

Where and When

Client: I'm on call to my boss 24/7. He calls me anytime, day or night. He is ADD-like, and if he thinks about it and it is important, he thinks it is important to everyone else.

I know other people in the office who are making more money than I am, and they work fewer hours. I think I need to leave. I just don't know where I would go. Plus there are perks to this job that I don't want to lose.

Therapist: What would it take financially and benefit-wise for you to no longer feel resentment knowing he is going to call you 24/7?

Client: Well, if I was making this amount and he did this for me, (I know he does it for someone else in the office), I could stay.

Therapist: Write that number down, whatever it is. Don't focus on any deals he might have made with someone else. Ask him to pick a time when you can talk about work, and let him know your thoughts. Put together several different scenarios, just in case he needs that kind of flexibility, but have the bottom line number in your head.

This client almost doubled her salary, and—far from feeling resentful—had a renewed motivation to be the best she could at her job.

When it comes to taking care of ourselves, we can't look to others and what they have or don't have: "She gets this, so I should have that." Instead, we must ask ourselves, "What is it that I need in order not to build resentment?" We also need to keep our emotions out of the conversation: "You like her better than me." Just make your request!

> **Client:** I make more money than my husband, and I'm constantly paying for things I don't tell him about. He'd be upset if he knew the actual cost. Even though he has no idea, I can still feel myself building up resentment, and I know I'm the culprit.

> **Therapist:** Do your homework. Figure out the expenses, make a budget, and decide what contribution you need from your husband.

Remember, if you are requesting something of a man in your life, be smart. Men like to solve problems. Don't get caught up with emotions, just make a clean request, like, "I need half of your paycheck every month, or I need all of your paycheck every month." And then set it up so that you don't have to ask every month, some sort of direct deposit, for example.

> **Client:** I think he'll be angry, because that number is a lot different from what I've accepted from him in the past.

> **Therapist:** It's easy to see in retrospect the messes we've made by not making a certain request sooner or by backing down from a request that we did make. And when we're working in the domain of money, there are going to be strong triggers for both people.

Remember these important distinctions: It's always more difficult to ask for change when it's a break in routine. If there's been a breakdown and we let that breakdown continue, we send the message that it's not a breakdown at all.

Then we have to own up and admit that we made a mistake: I let you think it was fine when, in fact, I've realized lately that it's not fine. I take responsibility for the past, but we need to start anew.

Identify the nature and difficulty of the conversation, and ask your partner to pick a time to talk. Present all the information, take responsibility for your part in the breakdown, and ask for what you need in order to not have resentment.

Let the other person have his say. Don't give up the conversation until you have resolution. It's OK to take breaks, but if you don't want to lose that person from your life, keep revisiting the issue until you have resolution.

In some cases, though, resolution means we've decided we're better off without a certain person in our lives.

Years ago, I was using an old school financial adviser. I would ask him why he chose a particular investment—what its advantage was over a different one, why not this one, what about that one. In other words, I insisted that he share with me the thinking behind his advice, not just his advice.

Finally, he said to me, "You're supposed to just do what I tell you," and that was the end of our relationship.

I also ended a relationship with a Harvard doctor, whom I actually liked in some domains. But when I would attempt a dialogue with him about a solution to a particular physical breakdown I was experiencing, he refused.

"I don't know why you come to me," he said. "You don't just do what I tell you to do."

You know who else told his clients to just do what he told them? Bernie Madoff.

Requests made in the financial domain are tough, but we need to be able to make them. Sometimes, they are as difficult as we would expect them to be, and other times, they are surprisingly simple.

> **Client:** I have three new clients in three different states! I get to work on new material, and I get to travel.
>
> Therapist: Have you had the money conversation with them? Do they know your fee?
>
> **Client:** No, but I'm sure it will work out. These are all good people.
>
> Therapist: No. Actually, it may not work out if you and they have a completely different idea of what your fee is.

Client: Asking for money is so hard for me. What if they change their minds and don't want to work with me?

Therapist: Why would you give your services away when you have all these unpaid bills?

Client: I don't feel worthy. I'm afraid they won't want to pay me.

Therapist: You are fabulous at what you do. Everyone is always telling you what a difference you've made in his or her life.

Remember this: People respect other people who respect themselves. This one idea is crucial to your success in life. You have actually managed to get through most of your life without making clean requests, and you have a history of feeling used and abused by people.

In spite of the fact that her requests sometimes went smoothly, this client continually struggled with asking for her fee. Sometimes, it would happen so easily that she was stunned, but nevertheless, she dreaded it and fretted that some requests might not be honored.

She always knew I was going to ask how her requests were going, and she knew it felt better when financial agreements were in place, but it continued to be a huge source of stress for her.

I recommended she hire someone to make the requests for her. We can't just pretend it doesn't matter. We either have to learn to ask for our money or hire someone to do it for us.

But you can't always hire someone. Take the most challenging request of all time, the Everest of requests, so to speak. What is it? Any request made in the sexual domain. Good luck hiring someone to do that for you!

Sex

So many men equate a negative response to requests in this area as a reflection of their inadequacy. Women know this, don't want to offend, and so say nothing.

What is the end result? The man eventually finds out or figures it out, but it's thirty, forty, or fifty years too late. Game, set, match—it's over, but no one's won. He lost and she lost, all because no one would bring it up. [37]

For new couples, I recommend giving thought to questions like these:

- *Are you a match sexually?*

- *Do you have similar sexual appetites?*

- *Can you both talk about sex?*

In this domain, I recommend focusing on the positive more than what isn't working.

If neither partner wants to discuss sex, there's no need to worry about a breakdown. But if one partner wants to talk about it and the other doesn't, "Houston, we have a problem."

The longer a couple has been together, and the longer any sexual patterns have manifested themselves, the more difficult it becomes to address or change those patterns.

Problems usually present themselves when one person deviates from the pattern or becomes dissatisfied with the status quo and isn't comfortable addressing it in conversation.

Pregnancy and the birth of a child can often change a sexual pattern. Sometimes, it's the man who might be nervous about having sex with his wife during pregnancy or after the birth of the child, and sometimes it's the wife who is "so exhausted" she has no interest in continuing their physical life. Do not pretend you don't have a breakdown! Pick a time agreeable to both of you and start talking about a resolution.

Problems always present themselves when one partner feels the other should know what she or he wants and that making such a request would spoil it.

Remember, none of us is a mind reader. We need to let our partner know what we want. Requests provide the people in our life with road maps as to how we want to be treated. Requests give our sexual partners a road map of how we would like our bodies to be treated.

We all grow and change, in all areas of life, not just sexually. It is not a sin to change, but it does present challenges if we are uncomfortable making requests.

Family Celebrations

Client: He did practically nothing for my birthday. He put a card by my morning cup of coffee. We always had such big birthday celebrations when I was growing up. We pretty much celebrated our birthdays for a week with different presents every day.

Therapist: What is his history of birthday celebrations? If he doesn't know yours, he will probably do what he's used to.

Client: I don't know.

Therapist: Sounds like a good conversation to have—the birthday conversation. Begin with an assessment of your histories: I liked this part, and I really didn't like that part. Then design how you want to celebrate your birthdays as a couple, and how you want to celebrate your children's birthdays.

This is a breakdown that can be handled with requests and negotiation. No one is wrong because they celebrated birthdays a certain way.

There is no bad guy here. There is simply, "Let's talk and figure out what we as a couple want to do." This conversation can be had for all family celebrations.

Homework

As homework, reflect on your history. If you grew up in a dysfunctional, addictive, abusive, or controlling family, for example, it may not have been safe to make requests.

If your childhood was about taking care of others, there may not have been room for requests.

Look at your life now. Do you live in an environment in which requests are tolerated?

Can you make requests of your friends and sexual partners, co-workers and employees, financial advisers, and mechanics?

Often, people-pleasers hate to make requests because they don't feel worthy. They are afraid of rejection. A typical people-pleaser request sounds something like this:

"There's a great movie playing tonight."

That's it. That's the request. Translation: "Mary, there's a great movie playing tonight. Would you like to go see it with me?"

Mary: "No, I can't. Thanks for asking. Maybe another time."

How great it would be if conversation were always that simple! It would be if we were all Sioux warriors.

"Stands With Fist, would you like to go to the movies with me tonight? There's a new slasher film I'm dying to see."

Stands With Fist: "No, I can't. Thanks for asking. Maybe another time."

Request Role Models

To become a warrior, we need role models like Stands With Fist. I got lucky. My role model happens to be a dear friend of mine. For him, making a request is truly as easy as a hot knife slicing through butter.

In spite of multiple surgeries, my friend became blind when he was just seventeen. I first met him when we were in our forties.

He was working two businesses, one on the East Coast, where he lived, and the other on the West Coast, so he traveled cross-country frequently. He had a wife, children, and a political appointment. He was a walking request.

When we went out to lunch, for example, he requested a synopsis of the menu. When the meal arrived, he requested specific placement of the food, for example, meat at 2 o'clock, please.

I loved being around him. He was authentic. He spoke his mind, and expected the same of those around him.

Requests Never Made

On the other hand, I worked with a woman who for two years had been sexually involved with a man who never once asked her out on a date.

They would both go drinking with respective friends, go home together at the end of the evening, and that's what they called dating.

But I didn't.

This client actually thought she wanted to spend her life with this man. I didn't think she even knew who he was as a friend, let alone as a life partner.

They had never really engaged in the game of life and love. He had never asked her to go to dinner, she had never asked him to pick her up, and so on. Given what life throws at families these days, I doubted that this couple was suitably prepared.

Make Those Requests!

Mutual request-making is one of the signs of a healthy marriage. It is our way of giving our significant other a road map of how to take care of us, because we are all different. We can't assume that what makes us happy necessarily makes our partner happy.

When we find ourselves complaining about how we are treated in the world, we have to look at our part in the dynamic. We not only have to require of ourselves that we make requests but we also have to look at whether our requests are being honored. Our requests let others know our standards. If we are honoring our standards, we should have few complaints about how we are treated in the world.

Fear of rejection often keeps us from making requests. One client in particular told me she would withdraw a request the second the other person hesitated.

We have to remember that when someone responds with a "No," it's no different than when we say "No" to them: It's not a rejection; it's an answer to a question. It is a statement about what you can or cannot do.

Make a list of where you think you are competent making requests and where you have difficulty. What do you notice?

- *Is your difficulty limited to the opposite sex?*

- *Is it with people you're close to?*

- *Is it money-related?*

- *Is it work-related?*

- *Is it in the domain of sex?*

Then consider why it's difficult with those people or in those situations. Here's a list of what other clients discovered about themselves:

- *I don't deserve to ask for anything.*

- *People who do that are selfish.*

- *Other people should be able to "mind read" and know what I want.*

- *My religious training taught me to only think of others.*

- *I need to be perfect before I can ask for something for me.*

- *People will know what you want, and they can harm you.*

- *People will know what you want, and they won't grant the request.*

- *If I know it's important to me, I'll be disappointed because there is no room for me to have requests.*

Pick a person or situation with whom or in which you think it will be easiest to make some headway. Begin to make requests in a restaurant if that feels comfortable. Notice what you tell yourself about asking the people close to you to do something. One woman reported how uncomfortable she felt when her husband did something really nice for her. This is called difficulty receiving!

You're Feeling Better, Aren't You, Honey?

Many women never realize that they've spoiled the people around them. When husbands and children become sick, mom's always there with chicken soup, ginger ale, and popsicles.

What a surprise it is to discover that when they themselves get sick, there's no one taking care of them.

If we haven't taught people to take care of us, we shouldn't be surprised when they don't.

Most families don't want to see Mother Earth on the couch, unable to serve them as she's done for years. How many of us have had our husbands ask, "You're feeling better, aren't you, honey?"

What he really wants to know is, "You're feeling good enough to start taking care of us again, aren't you?" Do not be disappointed because you expected the same people whom you yourself spoiled to take care of you when you yourself need taking care of.

I recommend, Mom, that if you are going to have surgery or you get sick—any situation where you need to count on others to take care of you—make requests of a community that you know can serve you. Ask a good friend, ask someone you pay—it's her job to make and bring you chicken noodle soup—but ask someone who you know will take care in the way you might do. Observe if you have difficulty receiving.

Our children don't need to see us as martyrs; they need to be taught many of the chores that make a family run. If you wear a cape with an S that stands for Supermom, it's time to engage the rest of the family. Here's how you might start:

"It is time for us to understand better how a family works. Certain things have to happen every day, and I think it's time for all of you to pick the things that you want to make happen every day. I've made a list, and I want you to pick off that list what you will do."

One client who tried this had two children, and she needed the groceries bought and the laundry done weekly. Each child picked what he would do.

She also told them they would have to do it together. They lived in a high rise in the city, where it was wise to be in groups rather than alone, so she felt safer if they were making a lot of noise together.

It also taught them to coordinate their action with that of other people. A child who wanted to be difficult and not get the groceries when the other child wanted to ran the risk of similar behavior when he wanted to do the laundry.

They did all the "fun" things kids do, such as push every button on the elevator when they got off (at the twentieth floor!) and bought groceries they wanted that weren't on the list, but they got everything done together.

With that one request alone, mom was able to take those things off her plate, and the kids actually "enjoyed" the time they had together.

Truth be told, they actually felt proud to be part of running the ship.

As these children matured and ventured out into the world, they met other people their age who had no idea how to take care of themselves in the domestic domain. The kids took further pride in teaching their skills to others.

Homework

Start making requests by vowing to make one per day, one per week, one per month, whatever you want. But whatever time frame you choose, stick to it.

Learning to make requests is not like learning to say No. There's no easing into it. Our only option is to go cold turkey.

For example, when we say, "Please don't," how does one ease into that? Our request is either honored or it's not. We either want a raise or we don't.

The only opportunity we have to ease into this learning process is the time frame to which we vow to adhere, so pick one that's reasonable for you and the type of relationships you are in.

Each time you make a request, see what sort of obstacles or reactions are present, and keep a journal noting the response if you observe:

• *Any of the feelings expressed in the list of what my clients found;*

> • *Physical reactions, such as voice stops working, knees shake, tears;*

> • *Verbal reactions, for example, if you withdraw the request.*

Note any specific people in your world who do not allow you to make requests. Note differences between making a request of one person versus asking another.

Remember to differentiate between chatter and physical reactions. Examples of chatter are: "You're not good enough. That's being selfish.

You're a bad person if you ask for things. What would your mother say? Don't rock the boat. Don't upset anyone."

Examples of physical reactions are queasy stomach, voice that shakes or stops, wobbly knees, tears, etc.

Decline the chatter and physical reactions, and make your request doing the salsa if necessary.

Take note of the feeling of strength and any other emotions when your first request is honored.

Success Story

Remember our young client who had been taken advantage of her whole life: She asked her new live-in boyfriend to put together a contract with her in which they both agreed to certain responsibilities. Her suffering vanished. She felt empowered in a way she had never felt before.

When you begin to clear the darkness and suffering you've lived with so easily, you start to wonder why it took you so long. These are just conversations! They are effective, powerful conversations, but they are just conversations.

Remember the young woman who suddenly realized she didn't have standards for the way people treated her. You practically have to get a certificate that you've passed standards to interact with her now.

Don't wait too long. When we start to regain our emotional health, we start to attract people who respect healthy people.

We begin to live a life where requests just flow, and before we know it, a time will come when we've just delivered ten requests and they were all granted or we survived the ones that were not. Requests will become transparent.

CHAPTER FOUR

SPEAKING AUTHENTICALLY

Keep Going

Let's start with a young woman who has a long history of failed relationships. She also has hurt people because she violated the rule you've heard me repeat over and over. She didn't give people the opportunity to fight for their relationship because she left it emotionally with another person.

After doing a lot of work, she now can bring up her concerns in a relationship, she doesn't bring in a third person, she can apologize and take responsibility for her mistakes, and she can still become paralyzed if someone throws her history at her: "You always hurt people. I knew you'd hurt me. Everyone told me you would hurt me."

When you don't feel good about yourself at your core, you are vulnerable to attacks by others. By developing your authentic self, you are building positive self-esteem and beginning to eradicate the core of negativity and self-doubt.

Remember our knuckle bleeding people-pleaser who could "cave" if someone attacked her ADD-like behavior or her hoarding. She rarely caves anymore.

Take a serious look at where you stand in the world.

• *Are your eyes wide open?*

• *Do you agree to what you know in your heart of hearts is wrong because you don't have a backbone?*

- *What do you want to say about yourself as you move through life? Do you want to stand for truth or lies?*

- *If you had the courage to say anything, what would it be?*

- *Are you still afraid of conflict?*

- *Do you still let people brainwash you for their own self-serving agenda?*

- *If you could relive certain times in your life, what would you have done differently?"*

- *What would you have said differently?*

- *Now that you have been working on declining what is not in your best interest and asking for what is, what do you see?*

- *What do you see about where you have been and where you are going?*

- *What do you notice different about your body?*

Remember Julie's mom, whose daughter asked, "Why can't you stand up to Alison's mom?" Well, now her daughter is saying, "Mom, you have courage. You're strong. You think something, you say it." How good must that feel!

When we are afraid, we cower. Our bodies shrink and our minds collapse, as mine did when I was mugged.

When we face the world as warriors, we unfold and expand.

Remember our knuckle-bleeding people-pleaser who now has standards? She likes to remember what it used to be like every now and then to appreciate what it feels like now. She knows the gifts of her knuckle-bleeding hard work: freedom from the incessant negative chatter, the absence of suffering, and an end to overcompensating, combined with her new sense of self, seeing her children act in healthier ways, and knowing it is a direct result of her.

Our young woman who said No to her boyfriend's need to see other people reported a surge of energy, newfound dignity, and a new belief in the person she is in the world.

Did these clients experience fear before having the new conversations or sadness if they didn't work out? Of course, and they can move through those feelings. When you keep taking actions that produce resentment, you don't move through the resentment, you live in it.

Many people report amazement at how fast they can move through issues that they used to suffer with for years.

Once we become warriors, life becomes easier, much easier.

For example, we have more energy because we have less anxiety.

I know one woman who has delightful dinner parties. At the end of the dinner, she thanks us all for coming, says she knows we would like to help clean up but that she likes to do it herself, and hopes we will all get together again soon.

The evening is over! She has boundaries and expresses them effortlessly, and no one ever has to guess when is the right time to leave.

Life also becomes easier as a warrior because we have more money. Why? Because we've said No to takers:

"I consider you a friend, so I'd like to give you the discounted family and friends rate" (but not free).

Life becomes easier as a warrior because we have fewer problems with our children. And they become better people, too, because we've become great role models.

Life is easier as a warrior. The hard part, however, is taking the steps to become one, and the most difficult step is before you now.

Learning to Speak Authentically

Research tells us people are more effective in their interpersonal interactions when they are more open and aware of their blindnesses. [38]

Research also tells us people feel more comfortable being open when they trust. Understanding cultures can help manage expectations and trust in relationships. We have the culture of our family of origin, the culture of our gender, our heritage, our geographical location, etc. An Italian male from New York lives in a different discourse with different expectations and standards than an adult female from El Salvador. We cannot assume everyone thinks the way we do. Trust increases the more we know about and understand others and ourselves. [39]

To achieve warriorhood, we need to learn to speak authentically. And that requires trust, respect, understanding of the person with whom we are speaking, and learning the steps needed to have a successful interaction.

Speaking authentically can be more difficult than declining and making requests. We will look at more challenging scenarios for this exercise. Some of the situations don't necessarily have a right answer, just a right answer for you. We are also going to look at situations where you might be dealing with more-difficult people.

People who are mentally fragile present different challenges. Often, they can dish out nastiness but crumble into hysterics or tears if you speak authentically to them. Some people we feel can "out-talk" us. How often have I heard, "She's smarter than I am. She gets louder and uses big words, and I get confused," etc. People who are controlling can become enraged if they feel the order they believe they need in the universe is threatened.

Let's look at some guidelines for you to remember as you begin the journey of being authentic by having authentic conversations.

Guidelines for Learning to Speak Authentically

Identify the conversation you would like to have before you start it, and both of you pick a time that is mutually convenient: "I'd like to have a talk about finances. What's a good time for you?"

> • *Take breaks if you get tired or overwhelmed, or just want one:? "This was a good start. Let's take a break and get back to the conversation tomorrow."*

> • *Avoid name-calling and personal attacks:? "You idiot. You're so stupid."*

- *Compliment whenever possible. Acknowledge the other person's strengths: "You're such a good father/husband/wife/friend." "You care about us. You are a good communicator."*

- *Apologize when it's called for: "I'm sorry I didn't bring this up earlier."*

- *"I apologize for attacking you. I shouldn't have."*

- *Avoid absolutes like "always" and "never": "You never compliment me." "You never help with the kids." "You're always working."*

- *Register complaints in a respectful way if you feel you must let the other person know what he or she is doing wrong. "I don't like it when you show up at our home without letting us know you're coming."*

- *Simply make your request or ask for the new behavior. "I'd like you to call us before you come over, and we can all decide what is a good time."*

- *Acknowledge the success of the conversation, negotiate, and/or agree to disagree.? "I understand that you want to come to our home whenever it's convenient for you, but that won't work. We'd like you to come two afternoons a week from three to five and two afternoons from two to five."*

There won't always be time to prepare each and every conversation you have. Life, as you know, just doesn't work like that. Remember the guidelines, and if it's possible to get the new behavior you're looking for without spending time on the behavior you don't like, that's best.

"Hi, I'd like to talk to you about something new our family is doing. From now on, we're asking people to call before they come over so we can all decide what are good times for visits."

The more you practice speaking authentically, the more likely it is that the words you have to choose in a pinch will embody the spirit of the language in the guidelines above and the examples below.

You can practice in the quiet of your home, with a partner or however you like. As a good place to start, we'll begin with some conversations that tend to trip people up.

Make sure you give yourself permission to speak authentically in situations you care about to an audience you believe can handle your authenticity. It's particularly important to give yourself permission to speak your truth in a situation where you are going to alter your behavior and do the opposite of what you promised.

For example, when most of us have a bad meal at a restaurant, we vow never to return—and also to tell everyone we know.

But what do we do in those cases when the server, host, or manager asks us how everything was? We say it was delicious and that we'll be back.

Speak up. The restaurant wants you to come back. Give its staff a chance to take better care of you.

Learning to speak authentically can be done in steps, which is to say we can practice in situations that are less demanding and in which less is at stake. Then we can work our way up to situations that are stressful and in which much more may be at stake.

For example, you might choose to start practicing at a restaurant you've never visited before, as opposed to one you frequent.

Real Life Examples 101

Waiter: How is everything cooked?

You: All the meals are perfect, except that I ordered my steak rare and it is medium.

Waiter: Thank you. We'll fix that immediately.

———

Doctor: I think I can fix your problem with surgery. I'm available to do it later this week. We have to move fast because I'm a very busy man.

You: Thank you for getting me in so quickly. What I'd like to do, though, is slow the process down a bit, take my records, and get a second opinion.

Doctor: Humph! Well, I may be too busy to see you by the time that happens.

———

You: Thank you for understanding what a major decision this is for me. I'd like to do my due diligence before signing on for surgery. Where can I get my records?

Landscaper: We can put all these trees close to the house for shade.

You: What if they grow so big they start to damage the house?

Landscaper: Oh, that won't happen.

You: Please put that in our agreement. It might take years for the trees to grow that big, and this way, both of us will have a record of it.

You (later): Hi, we have a problem because what I was concerned about is now a reality. The roots of the trees are damaging the house. I'm glad we wrote the agreement to include this concern.

———

Plumber: Well, that should take care of everything. You should have hot water with no problems.

You: And if for some unknown reason, I'm standing in a cold shower, what's your warranty for your work, and let's get that in writing.

———

Contractor: I'll be in charge of making sure everything gets done correctly and on budget, and for that, you pay me ten percent of the total cost.

You: What I'd like to do is sit down every week with you, go over what happened that week, what didn't happen and why, and where we are with the budget.

———

Financial adviser: You just give us your money, and we'll handle it from there.

You: I am a person who has gone from never asking questions to asking a million, so let me know if your firm can accommodate an interested investor who wants to stay on top of his portfolio by speaking with my contact person. If you don't work that way, I'll find someone who does. Thank you.

———

Business you're signing a contract with: OK, I'll have all the paperwork drawn up by Monday for you to sign. Then we can move forward and you'll give us your deposit.

You (after obtaining new information and changing your mind): We've done further research and found someone who fits our parameters better. We have decided to sign on with their agency. We appreciate all the time you took with us. Thank you.

———

Dead-beat boyfriend: What do you mean where are we going? We're just hanging out and having fun.

You: Call me if and when you get a plan. (Read Steve Harvey's book: Act Like a Lady, Think Like a Man)

———

Eye-roving boyfriend: Whew! She's hot!

You: Call me when you get your eyes fixed!

———

Controlling husband wanting fast divorce: You know we've grown apart. I'll have my lawyer draw up a settlement and you can just sign it.

You: Actually, no, I didn't know we'd grown apart. Is there any chance we can get help to fix our thirty-year marriage? If not, please send me an offer and I'll review it with my team and get back to you.

————

Ex-wife/ex-girlfriend: I need you here Saturday morning at nine to help me load up these heavy things and take them to the dump. I don't have anyone else, and I really need help.

You: Actually, that's not going to work for me. Thanks for asking.

————

Ex-wife/ex-girlfriend: I need you to be my escort at the office party this year. We can go as friends, and no one has to know. I just don't want to go alone. We had plans to go before we broke up, and everyone is expecting you to go. Please.

You: Actually, that's not going to work for me. Thanks for asking.

————

Unconsciously controlling friend: I signed us up for the course I want to do this weekend. Pick me up on Friday at five.

You: Thanks, but I won't be able to make it.

————

Difficult parent in long-term care: Do you know I'm always alone here on Sunday? All the other residents are out for dinner with their children. I'm the only one here who never gets calls. Did you forget you had a mother? So you finally found your way here.

You: Hi, Mom! Let's go for a walk.

————

Disapproving parent: Are you really going to leave your secure corporate job to start your own business?

You: Yes, and I hope you're happy for me, because I'm really happy!

————

Disapproving child to parent: What do you mean you're moving to the islands? Who's going to babysit for us?

You: I'm so excited about moving to the islands. It will be such fun when you visit.

————

Abusive partner: I'll teach you to never look at another man/woman again. Smack!

You: 911—I have an emergency at 99 West Drive. Please come immediately!

————

Lawyer's office: You must stay away from this abusive partner, and you must testify!

You: I will and I will!

Advanced Real Life Examples

I have had many examples of families that unknowingly keep their children dependent on them by enabling their children's addictions. Some parents keep their children on the payroll and attach conditions to the money. Others forget that their children have grown up and don't live in their home anymore. As your children are growing up, your job as a parent continues to change. You must be encouraging your children to find their voice even if it is different from your voice.

If you as a parent want to contribute to your children financially, you must do so without strings attached. Giving your children money doesn't give you a ticket to make their decisions for them. You had your turn to raise your family, and now, you must let your children raise their children!

This does not mean that parents of grown children can never have an opinion about their children's families. It does not mean that children must exclude their parents from important decisions they are making.

If everyone is healthy and subscribes to autonomy, these conversations will be easy. There are plenty of philosophies on how to raise our children today.

There also are lots of difficult waters to negotiate as a parent. Decisions need to be made about health, education, discipline, athletics, you name it—so why not discuss these issues with someone you respect and who has already been down this road? Yes, discuss, but it is the grown child's final decision, with his or her spouse.

If you have overbearing, intrusive, controlling parents, you may need to set firm boundaries: "Thanks for sharing, Mom and Dad. We'll take it from here."

If children on the other hand expect their parents to continue supporting them after they are married, parents may have to set the boundaries. One parent told me he thought the greatest gift he could give his children was to take care of himself so they wouldn't have to.

Parents, give because you have extra and you want to, not because you are a martyr or want to control your children.

Let me be clear on what I'm saying. I believe close families with healthy boundaries that support autonomy are what our families and our country need today. In no way am I against close families. I just advocate that they be emotionally healthy families.

Parents

Client: The only relatives that live anywhere close to us are impossible. They show up whenever it's convenient for them, with no regard for what we are doing.

They stir the pot by getting involved in difficult conversations we are having with the children. My husband and I are at our wits' end.
He thinks we have to take a really tough stand, and I don't know if I'm up to it. I keep telling myself that they're family, and maybe we're being too mean.

Therapist: If you and your husband are beginning to fight about this issue, then it's time to get on the same side. You have to set boundaries with people who are unhealthy for your family.

This will be very tough for you, because you don't like to hurt people and you want everyone to like you. I encourage you to stand united as a couple and use words like "we," "my husband and I," and "my wife and I."

You will have to decide what to do if they ignore what you ask them to do and disrespect your boundaries. What will you do if you ask them to come on Tuesdays from three to five p.m., and they come on Monday or won't leave at five on Tuesday?

Client: My husband says we have to be prepared to close the door on them or usher them out. He says he'll do it if it's too hard for me.

Therapist: He is really being a partner to you in this breakdown. You need to be able to support him when he does the tough stuff. You can't go against him in front of your relatives. Don't even start the conversation until you are totally united—no matter what antics they pull.

Client: I can already imagine them telling the rest of the family how horrible we are, and how they just wanted to get together as family.

Therapist: And ….

Client: I know, I know. I still want everyone to like me.

How do we handle volatile situations that require us to make tough decisions?

Two great examples of phenomenal child-rearing are Anne Sullivan in The Miracle Worker [40]and Ray Charles's mother in Ray. [41]

Neither could afford to be people-pleasers. Sullivan had to prepare Helen Keller for dealing with her deafness and blindness. Her commitment and integrity are so poignantly illustrated in the famous dinner scene where Anne confronts Helen's equally determined temper tantrums. Ray's mom, who had to prepare him for his blindness, demonstrates her commitment and tough love with the powerful scene in which she says, "I'll show you how to do something once. I'll help you if you mess up twice. But the third time, you're on your own. 'Cause that's how it is in the world."

Their courage, caring, and perseverance made a real difference. Compare their actions with those of Cartman's mom in South Park.

Divorce

Client: My best friend is getting divorced, and she and her husband have always been our best friends. She's asked me to never talk to her husband again because he has been so mean to her. What do I do? We don't support what her husband, who's also our friend, has done to her either, and it's a real conflict for us.

On top of it all, our children all hang out, so we're going to be at ball games together. It's not just about us. We want to do what's in the best interest of the kids.

Therapist: These situations never have one right answer. I think the best you can do is to go through a healthy process of thinking through your decisions.

For instance, what is your friend trying to accomplish by asking you to never talk to her husband? Is there a different way to accomplish this goal? Is your friend asking you to never speak to her ex about how she is doing? You can certainly honor that. It's not your job to carry information about either partner to the other one.

She may need a safe or comfortable place to react to this trauma. Both of you can also certainly let her husband know what you think about his behavior, and that you in no way condone how he has left his marriage: affair, financial abandonment, lies, deserting his children.

Since the children are young adults, you can have your own conversation with them: "I'm sorry you're going through this divorce. We don't support your dad's moving on so fast, and understand that it might be hard for you. We just want you to know we are here for you if you need to talk or are just having a bad day."

These are difficult situations, particularly in a small town. Ask questions to help sort out how you can be most sensitive to the needs of your friends and their family.

The most important concept here is that if you only people-please, you will just do what you're told without thinking. A better solution is for you and your spouse to sit down and discuss your values, thoughts, and ideas about the requests being made of you and to come up with a solution that works for your family.

Don't forget that respect and sensitivity are just as important to living with dignity as is speaking honestly.

Remember the Indians in Dances With Wolves for whom confrontations were always resolved in a way that allowed all parties to retain their dignity?

Surround yourself with people who welcome authentic conversations.

Recognize the people in your life who can't handle authentic conversations. It will be up to you to determine where they fit in your life. Sometimes, there are people who can't handle authentic conversations whom we still must keep in our lives, e.g., family, teachers, coaches, bosses, etc. Create boundaries. Set up the situations for success, e.g., having buffers, interacting around safe, structured activities, and recognizing that these can be difficult to deal with. One wise client who had become quite competent in having authentic conversations also had many challenging family gatherings, which he could not resolve with authenticity. He finally realized he would have to just love his family, take care of himself during the get-togethers, and vent when they were over.

Now that you have been working toward warriorhood, what are you finding out about yourself?

- *What do you notice about where you've been and where you're going?*

- *Is anything different about your mindset?*

- *Has your body changed?*

- *Have you noticed a surge of energy when you say No to whomever or whatever won't support you, and Yes to taking a stand?*

Homework

For homework, journal your thoughts, your new practices, your reactions, what you're learning, and what is different in your body. One way to help yourself on the path of authentic living is to write standards for yourself:

• *Do you want people around you who can speak the truth, or are you still comfortable with elephants on the table, burping, farting, and throwing up?*

• *Do you want people close to you who don't keep their agreements?*

• *Do you want people close to you who don't call you back?*

• *Do you want people close to you who only want you to agree with them?*

• *Do you want people close to you who "brainwash" and "use" you for their own insecure, self-serving needs?*

• *Do you want people close to you who steamroll you and your opinions?*

• *Do you want people close to you who never question you?*

• *Do you want people close to you who never ask you about you?*

• *Do you want people close to you who only tell you what you want to hear?*

Think about our heroes: the Liberian women, the Afghan Olympian, the young girls in Afghanistan pursuing their education in spite of having acid thrown in their faces. They have set standards for themselves that they were willing to risk their lives for.

In 2002, three American heroes of mine risked not their lives but certainly their way of life to stand up for what they believed.

• Coleen Rowley of the FBI;

• Sherron Walkiuns of Enron;

• Cynthia Cooper of World.com.

Each had the courage to go against the tide and say that enough is enough.

Kudos to Time magazine for making them 2002's "Persons of the Year." What these women said was not popular or well received. Time recognized them for their integrity.

On a scale of 1-10, these women are a 10. Where do you put yourself? Where do you want to be? Let's get going!

CHAPTER FIVE

EMBRACE POSITIVE CHANGE

Compassion for Missed Opportunity

While writing this book, I actually sat in a car with the engine running while the driver filled it up with gas because I couldn't think of what to say or do: Should I just leap over the seat and turn it off? Jump out of the car (and say what)? Open the window and ask that the car be turned off? Game over: The driver was back inside, the gas tank was filled, and we were on our way. I did not bring up my concern for the next thirty minutes we were driving. No success but lots of learning.

Hang On in the Bumps

Remember the little girl whose mom said that if she made a request of her dad, he would hit her? Well, not all requests have that horrible outcome, but they also may not be met with open arms.

- *I remember asking something of a service man whose response was to yell at me.*

- *A parent I know made a totally appropriate request of her teenage daughter whose response was to start yelling at her hysterically.*

- *A man's request that his wife kiss him hello and goodbye and have conversations with him in the evening was met with, "You want so much from me. I can never do enough for you. You are so demanding."*

• *A woman's request that her husband plan his vacation with the guys in a way that would be best for the family was met with, "Why do you always do this to me?"*

These irrational responses are just that: irrational. All the requests were appropriate, reasonable, and doable. Don't stop making requests because of other people's irrational responses. You have the right to make requests!

The same can be true for declining requests and having authentic conversations. You are not always going to get rational responses. Begin to weed out the people who can't play at the emotionally healthy level you want to play at. Don't give emotionally unhealthy behavior the power to keep you stuck!

Remember the Success Stories

Do I really want to go through this, you ask yourself, and why? Remember our first chapter on why it is so important to have tools for self-advocacy.

The world is a more-complicated place to live in. Having just one tool called "people-pleasing" is not enough.

There are different levels of becoming a warrior. First and foremost is your own personal world. Cleaning out your resentment drawer is the first line of business. Take a look at the domain of finances. Are there areas where you can stop the money from going out and request that more money come in? Remember our young woman who almost doubled her salary by one request conversation. How about the married women who now have more financial equality?

Move next to the domain of love. If you are single, there are lots of great books to read, e.g., Steve Harvey's *Act Like a Lady, Think Like a Man*, and most of them are asking you to develop standards for yourself. It's time! If we women require our men to be the best they can be, everyone wins!

Take a look at resentments you might have with your family. Find your voice! Remember Julie's words to her mother: "Mom, you have courage. You're strong. You think something, you say it."

Make requests of your children. Say No to being taken advantage of. Remember our mom who with one request took laundry and shopping off her plate. Remember how proud her children were of contributing to the family. Allow your children the joy of being part of the family's success.

Hopefully, you are not in an abusive relationship, but if you are, please say No to the abuse. The only appropriate response from the abuser to a 911 call by the victim is, "Thank you. I might have really hurt you. Thank you for stopping me." One young couple is healing together because the abuser said, "Thank you for getting me help before it was too late." Remember, the only appropriate response from the abuser if you call 911 to report the abuse is, "Thank You"!

Find balance in your life. Say No to martyr, victim, and overworking! Say Yes to healthy eating, exercise, grounding practices, and, for openers, anything else that supports your living in joy, love, peace, courage, contentment, and passion.

It is up to you to choose the level of warrior you want to become. Start with your own personal world, and live in it resentment-free. If you have a passion or cause that gets your juices going, move on out into the world, where lots of warriors are taking a stand against its darkness.

Frolic or Struggle?

Balancing between new and old behavior can be like entering the surf. I remember one particular day in Lanai when getting in the water was like being tossed around in life. If you tried to muscle your way, determined to stand your ground, you were either dumped unceremoniously onto the beach by large incoming waves or dragged out underwater into the ocean by a strong outgoing wave.

Everyone played in the waves in different ways. One young child leaped up and hit the wave with his backside. A young couple clung together and let the waves toss them around. Some people dove through the waves, some dove under the waves, and some dove up and over the waves.

One woman with a snorkel on who swam into shore from about a half-mile out was an inspiration to watch. She kept her head down and just went on swimming "by feel." When she felt she was swimming forward and going backward, she didn't panic but just waited patiently for the next wave and began swimming with it toward the beach. There are times we find ourselves going against the flow of life when we all need to wait patiently until we can go forward with the flow again.

In addition, if you trusted the process of floating over the incoming waves, letting the strong outgoing waves carry you to the calm ocean beyond, it all worked perfectly. The same was true of riding the flow back onto the beach. At one moment, knowing I was so close to the beach but still not feeling any ground under me, I panicked, almost going into the muscling process. "No, no, no, all is well. Trust," a voice said, as I went back into the flow of the ocean to be gently dropped onto the beach.

The same day, a school of spinner dolphins hung out all day in the water with us. Their playful frolicking served as a reminder of how we can play in life. Do you want to choose effort and struggle or dance and frolic? It's up to you!

THE BACKBONE WORKBOOK

WORKBOOK INTRODUCTION

Learning in a group can be very powerful. Back in the '80s, many of us were so excited about what Dr. Fernando Flores was teaching us that we would drive hours to participate in our group and do the exercises. We were men and women busy in our careers and raising our families, yet we knew that if we embraced this learning, we would be more effective in every area of our lives. We took the time we didn't have and reaped the rewards, forever different in the world.

Find committed people and bring your own commitment. Study, observe, discuss, and do the practices with rigor. Begin to bring requests, the ability to say No, and your authentic conversations into your everyday life. Discuss your resistance, your breakthroughs, your learning, and your successes, and keep moving.

You can bring dignity into your life and change how you are in the world with repetition and practice. As you become more comfortable, up the ante and make the topic of the conversations more difficult.

Bring the same rigor to your commitment to your body as well. Work in a group with a trainer until you have changed your practices to those that support your goals for a healthy, strong body.

And finally, do the same for your spiritual foundation. Develop practices that help you when your world turns upside down. Have in place your moral compass, your how-to-make-sense-when-life-doesn't-make-sense, and the beliefs and practices that bring you peace and help you make sense of the world.

Honor yourself for your hard work, successes, and perseverance. Notice how much easier life is and how much energy you now have to live.

Notice how passionate you are about life. Notice how others want to be around you with your newfound confidence and clarity.

Remember our spinner dolphins.

FAMILY OF ORIGIN WORK

Attend a Family of Origin Treatment Program, such as Survivors I at the Meadows in Wickenburg, Arizona.

Hire a qualified Backbone coach to help you with the group work. (For more information, go to www.backbonepower.com)

Gather your group and go through all of the exercises in the workbook.

KNOW YOUR EMOTIONAL HISTORY

Activity One: Draw a genogram for yourself to see themes, deaths, suicides, depression, illnesses, drugs, and alcohol use, and the significant players as you were growing up.

Activity Two: Make two lists, Fear and Love. Identify the behaviors of Mom and Dad that elicited Fear or Love in you. For example: Mom afraid of her critical, controlling, judgmental self, and loving us through cooking and cleaning; Dad afraid of his rage both yelling and hitting, and loving us through providing.

Activity Three: Answer the above questions for siblings, grandparents, aunts, uncles, cousins, teachers, coaches, and anyone else who was significant in your life from birth until around age 21:

For example: Grandmother on Dad's side, cold and giving us everything materially; Grandmother on Mom's side, loving us unconditionally ... our milk and cookies grandmother.

Ask yourself how you coped with behaviors that made you fearful. For example: I tried to be perfect; I became the black sheep; I studied really hard to get straight A's; I did everything I was told; I was compliant; I was a good boy; I became the best athlete; I tried to please everyone; I acted out; I stayed away from home, etc.

```




```

Ask yourself if you could buck the system or say No anywhere (not about going to bed, eating your meals, etc., but about things that might be a choice). Did one parent let you, did both, or did neither allow you choices? How did you cope if the answer was No? (I pretended I didn't care, for example.)

```




```

Ask yourself if you could safely make requests, and if so, were some honored or was that a scary idea? What did your parents do with requests from their children? How did you cope if the answer was No? (I pretended I didn't have any requests, for example.)

```




```

Ask yourself if your family valued authentic conversations. Could you register your upsets? How was anger handled? How did you cope? (For example, I tried to disappear, I was always at other people's homes, or I played sports.)

Discuss each family member in the context of love, fear, saying No, making requests, and having authentic conversations. Discuss how you coped and what you learned and didn't learn. As a group, help each other unravel the mystery of your heritage. You are not doing therapy; you are just working to understand where you came from, what tools you were given, and what tools you need.

Recommendations:

Hire a results-orientated coach or therapist who can make observations and give constructive feedback about the gifts and challenges of your family of origin.

Begin to identify your strengths and challenges in saying No, making requests, and speaking authentically. Look at all the worlds you live in today, e.g., career, family, friends, and love, and ask yourself if it is safe to say No, make requests, and speak authentically.

Notes

KNOW YOUR PHYSICAL HISTORY

Activity One: What Were You Taught? What were you taught about eating in your family of origin? Were you taught to value your body? Was food used to attempt to appease emotions? What did your parents teach you about health and exercise, and what did they actually do? Were there any role models for health, being physically fit, good posture, eating well, avoiding excess, using moderation, working out, avoiding addictions, etc.

Activity Two: Now, how about you today?

Do you work out?   Yes _____   No _____

How do you carry yourself physically?

Do you have extra weight for protection, because you fell asleep at the wheel of life, because you numb yourself with food, because you are trapped in the people-pleasing discourse, and if you are going to please all those people, you need some rewards for you, because you are unhappy, because you are an emotional eater, and on and on?

> _____
> _____
> _____
> _____
> _____

How have your conversations changed if you gained weight?

> _____
> _____
> _____
> _____
> _____

Do you want your weight or body to be different?

> _____
> _____
> _____
> _____
> _____
> _____

What healthy habits do you have or not have?

> _____
> _____
> _____
> _____
> _____
> _____

How do you think you carry yourself?

>

What goals do you want to set for yourself with the group's support?

>

What action are you willing to take today?

>

Recommendations:

- Take a Model Mugging class together as a group.
- Sign up for a martial arts class.
- Pick a healthy way of eating that you will adopt as a lifestyle, not a "diet." Hire a coach or professional who can guide you through changing your eating habits in a way that works for you financially and time-wise.
- Work out, run, or walk as a group or in small groups. Pick an activity and do it regularly with a partner, part of your group, or your entire group.

- Begin to stand up straight, pay attention to your posture, walk with dignity, sit with dignity during your group, do anything that calls attention to a new posture of "don't mess with me." Walk with a purpose, sit with a purpose, live with a purpose, and support each other in this mindset at all times.
- What do you notice week to week??Discuss what blocks you have, what chatter in your head changes, how you are different as you make physical changes. Some people who begin to lose weight experience fear of being vulnerable. Observe what you do as you become more physically fit.?
- Pick a physical goal as a group, e.g., a marathon or bike race, hiking a long trail or up a mountain. Train together. Journal your journey!

Notes

KNOW YOUR SPIRITUAL HISTORY

Activity One: What were you taught by your family of origin about having a spiritual or religious life?

What practices did your family have?

Did you participate?   Yes _____   No _____

What did you believe?

Did your beliefs help you when times were difficult?

Yes ___ No ___

Discuss with your group.

Activity Two: Where are you now? What do you believe about life and how it works?

```
_____
_____
_____
_____
_____
_____
_____
```

Do you have an internal private life?   Yes ___ No ___

Do you believe in something or someone bigger than yourself?

Yes ___ No ___

```
_____
_____
_____
_____
```

Do you understand that all the answers come from within?

Yes ___ No ___

```
_____
_____
_____
_____
```

Do you understand that nothing external will ever heal anything internal? Do you understand that the most powerful people have a strong sense of peace, joy, and gratitude coming from within?

Yes ___ No ___

Begin to explore in your group different spiritual discourses. Identify what you want from a spiritual life. Support each other in finding the perfect discourse and practices for you. Go to a bookstore as a group and identify books that will support you on this path. Read and discuss them as a group. Do not people-please here. What is it that you need and want for a spiritual life? Don't rush this process. Your faith and spiritual life can assist you during the toughest times, increase the joy in your life, and help you make sense of the last chapter of our lives.

Activity Three: Watch and discuss these movies with your group:

- *Dances With Wolves*

- *Forrest Gump*

- *Pray the Devil Back to Hell*

- *The Miracle Worker*

- *Ray*

Whom do you identify with and why?

```
_____
_____
_____
_____
_____
```

Who is your role model and why?

```
_____
_____
_____
_____
_____
```

What do you notice about your body when you are watching someone you respect?

```
_____
_____
_____
_____
_____
_____
```

What do you notice about your body when you are watching the warriors resolve conflict with dignity?

```
_____
_____
_____
_____
_____
_____
```

What do you notice about your body when you are watching Jenny in Forrest Gump before she throws the stones?

Do you think Anne Sullivan is mean during the dinner scene with Helen Keller?

Discuss the power of "group" as it relates to Pray the Devil Back to Hell and as it relates to your group.

- Find a movie that is inspirational to you as an individual and as a group. Watch and discuss the movie.
- Begin to find inspirational role models for yourselves.

Notes

LET'S GO TO WORK!

Activity One: Begin a people-pleasing journal, writing down all the areas where you were not true to yourself.

Activity Two: Make a list of your competences.

Activity Three: List areas in which you want to be competent but feel you are not.

Activity Four: List what you like about yourself.

Activity Five: List what you don't like about yourself.

Activity Six: Notice if you use your incompetence or what you don't like about yourself to justify your people-pleasing. Discuss this with your group.

Notes

SAYING NO SUCCESSFULLY

Activity One: Answer the following:

Do you say No to your children, your spouse, your friends, your co-workers, people who ask you to do or give things you can't or don't want to?

Yes ___ No ___

Do you say No to doctors, therapists, lawyers, contractors, electricians, plumbers, teachers?

Yes ___ No ___

Do you say No to unwanted sex or requests for money that don't serve you?

Yes ___ No ___

Activity Two: Observe and discuss with your group all the areas in which you are asked to do things and can't say No.

Observe how this contributes to your being competent in doing more than others because your normal has become so high. For example, you work eighty hours to other people's forty, you serve on twelve boards to others' three, you baby-sit everyone's children, you don't want to say No to others at the expense of yourself.

Observe and discuss where you have resentment and why you told yourself you couldn't say No.

Discuss with the group what you experience when someone says No to you.

Do you feel rejected?

Practice saying No with your group until you don't experience rejection.

Discuss with your group why you think saying No is "wrong."

Activity Three: Observe if you use stories to say No. Discuss why. If you need to begin with "I don't know," look at how that serves you.

Begin to set up scenarios you can practice with your group. Have the members make requests of you to which you must say No without stories. Watch your body's reactions. You must answer with No and thank you for asking. No stories and lots of repetition and practice.

Notes

MAKING REQUESTS
SUCCESSFULLY

Activity One: Answer the following:

Can you make requests of your spouse, children, friends, co-workers, and anyone else you need something from?

Yes ___ No ___

Can you make requests of the people you pay for their services, e.g., doctors, therapists, lawyers, electricians, plumbers, and contractors?

Yes ___ No ___

Can you make requests in the domain of sex and/or money?

Yes ___ No ___

Activity Two: Review your history and look at whether you were able to make requests.

- Observe and discuss with your group the story you have about why requests are bad.
- Observe and discuss with your group the areas where you have resentment.
- Observe and discuss the domains where you have let people believe the status quo is fine with you when it isn't.

Do you have areas where it is not safe to make requests? Can you leave these situations?

Discuss this with your group, and get appropriate help if necessary.

Discuss with the group and set up scenarios to support you in becoming competent in this area of making requests. Make clear requests stating the name of the person to whom the request is directed and that you are asking something of the person.

Notice your body's reaction as you train to make the request. Notice any resistance, breakdowns, and successes.

Notes

SPEAKING AUTHENTICALLY

Activity One: List conversations you wished you had had in the past.

List conversations you wish you could have now.

Activity Two: Review the examples in Chapter 4.

Activity Three: Guidelines for Having Authentic Conversations

• Identify the conversations you would like to have, and work with the person to find a mutually convenient time.

• Take breaks if you get tired or overwhelmed, or just want a break.

• Avoid name-calling and personal attacks.

• Compliment whenever possible.

• Acknowledge the other person's strengths.

• Apologize when it is indicated.

• Avoid absolutes like "always" and "never."

• Register complaints, if necessary, in a respectful way.

• Just make your request for the new behavior.

• Acknowledge the success of the conversation, negotiate, and/or agree to disagree.

Notes

INCREASING THE WARRIOR JUICES

Activity One: Discuss in your group how you would handle different scenarios. Role-play.

Activity Two: Change the fear juice into warrior juice.

Activity Three: Look at taking stands for integrity and speaking our truth.

Crisis management example: You are a web designer and are asked by your boss to design a website for a client that is degrading to women. You love your job and the people you work with, but you can't do what your boss has asked. How do you handle this? (The actual designer told her boss she would do it only if he would show the result to his mother and daughter.)

Be creative with your challenging examples, and look for creative ways to handle them. Begin to get excited about these situations rather than afraid of them.

Practice with your group. Go over all the conversations of the group, and get people's feedback. Have these conversations until you feel comfortable, and then design new, more-difficult conversations. Practice those conversations until you feel comfortable.

Notes

WRAPPING UP!

When you have completed the book and/or workbook, think about setting up a committed network of support. Find people who support your being different in the world, and set up a regular time to talk and discuss your progress with them.

- *Are you on track with your goals?*
- *What is in the way if not?*

Acknowledge your successes, and keep raising the bar. Surround yourself with people who want to grow and are committed to your doing the same. Be a committed person for others. Do not be a people-pleaser and tell others what you think they want to hear. Do not have people-pleasers in your network of support. You need honest feedback from competent, committed people.

Notes

RESOURCES

www.backbonepower.com

Breakthrough at Caron, 1-800-268-6529
www.breakthroughatcaron.org

The Hoffman Process, 1-800-632-3697

www.hoffmaninstitute.org

The Meadows, Survivors I, 1-800-632-3697

Onsite Living Centered Program, 1-800-341-7432

www.onsiteworkshops.com

END NOTES

Introduction

1. Donna F. Lamar, Transcending Turmoil: Survivors of Dysfunctional Families (New York: Plenum Press, 1997), 176.

2. Lamar, 176.

3. Dances With Wolves, directed by Kevin Costner. Tig Productions, 1990.

4. Forrest Gump, directed by Robert Zemeckis. Paramount Pictures, 1994.

5. Searle, Speech Acts: An Essay in the Philosophy of Language (Cambridge: Cambridge University Press 1969), 31.

6. Harriett Rubin, "The Power of Words," Fast Company, No. 21 (December 31, 1998).

Chapter 1

7. Harry Levinson, The Great Jackass Fallacy (Cambridge: Harvard University Press, 1973), 36.

8. Levinson, The Great Jackass Fallacy, 39-40.

9. Claire Raines and Lara Ewing, The Art of Connecting: How to Overcome Differences, Build Rapport, and Communicate Effectively With Anyone (New York: Amacon, 2006), 111-115.

10. Seth Allcorn, Codependency in the Workplace: A Guide for Employee Assistance and Human Resource Professionals (New York: Quorum Books, 1992), 14.

11. Dances With Wolves, directed by Kevin Costner. Tig Productions, 1990.

12. W.S.F. Pickering and Geoffrey Walford, Durkheim's Suicide: A Century of Research and Debate (United Kingdon: Routledge, 2000), 11-20.

13. Mary Anne La Torre, "Meditation and Psychotherapy: An Effective Combination," Perspectives in Psychiatric Care 37, No. 3 (2001): 103.

14. Carlos A. Arnaldo, ed., Child Abuse on the Internet: Ending the Silence (New York: Berghaha Books, 2001), 7.

15. Arnaldo, 68.

16. Ann J. Cahill, Rethinking Rape (New York: Cornell University Press, 2001), 16.

17. The Oprah Winfrey Show, February 8, 2010.

18. Cahill, 19.

19. Judith S. Wallerstein and Joan B. Kelly, Surviving the Breakup: How Children and Parents Cope With Divorce (New York: Basic Books, 1996), 55-75.

20. Wallerstein, Surviving the Breakup: How Children and Parents Cope With Divorce, 77.

21. Pray the Devil Back to Hell, directed by Abigail E. Disney and Gini Reticker, Fork Films, 2008.

22. "Verbatim," Time (February, 2, 2009): 20.

Chapter 2

23. Elizabeth A. Skowron, Stephen R. Wester, and Razia Azen, "Differentiation of Self Mediates College Stresses and Adjustment," Journal of Counseling and Development 84, No. 1 (2004): 69.

24. Allison Callaway, Deaf Children in China (Washington: Gallaudet University Press, 2000), 37.

25. Leonard Zusne and Warren H. Jones, Anomalistic Psychology: A Study of Magical Thinking (New Jersey: Lawrence Erlbaum Associates, 1989), 13-15.

26. Seth Allcorn, Codependency in the Workplace: A Guide for Employee Assistance and Human Resource Professionals (New York: Quorum Books, 1992), 11.

27. Pray the Devil Back to Hell, Abigail E. Disney and Gini Reticker, Fork Films, 2008.

28. Einat Peled, Zvi Eisikovits, Guy Enosh, and Zeev Winstok, "Choice and Empowerment for Battered Women Who Stay: Toward a Constructivist Model," Social Work 45, No. 1 (2000): 9.

29. Renee Brant, "Case Vignette: Child Abuse or Acceptable Cultural Norms," Ethics & Behavior 5, No. 3 (1995): 283.

30. Talking Heads. Once in a Lifetime on Remain in Light (audio CD). Burbank, Ca: Distributed by Warner Brothers, 1980.

31. Kandra Strauss, "Dumping the Stress by Getting Fit," National Education Association 20, No. 7 (April 2002): 35.

32. John P. Miller, The Contemplative Practitioner: Meditation in Education and the Professions (Connecticut: Bergin & Garvey, 1994) 51-54.

Chapter 3

33. Colin Feltham and Windy Dryden, Brief Counseling: A Practical, Integrative Approach (England: Open University Press, 2006), 145-146.

34. Kimberly Davis, "Making Blended Families Work," Ebony 55, No. 12 (October 2000): 40.

35. "McGraw's Search for His Father," The Week (November 13, 2009): 10.

36. Judith S. Wallerstein and Joan B. Kelly, Surviving the Breakup: How Children and Parents Cope With Divorce (New York: Basic Books, 1996), 77.

37. Karen Winkler, "Kinsey, Sex Research, and the Body of Knowledge: Let's Talk About Sex," Women's Studies Quarterly 33, No. ¾ (2005): 285.

Chapter 4

38. Timothy J. Galpin and Mark Herndon, The Complete Guide to Mergers and Acquisitions: Process Tools to Support M&A Integration at Every Level (San Francisco: Jossey-Bass, 2000), 93-95.

39. Karola Alford, "Gender Culture in a Relationship Workshop for College Students," Journal of College Counseling 4 No. 1 (2001): 85

40. The Miracle Worker, Arthur Penn. Playfilm Productions, 1962.

41. Ray, Taylor Hackford, Bristol Bay Productions, 2004.

BIBLIOGRAPHY

1. Alford, Karola. Gender Culture in a Relationship Workshop for College Students, Journal of College Counseling, 4 No. 1 (2001): 85.
2. Allcorn, Seth. Codependency in the Workplace: A Guide for Employee Assistance and Human Resource Professionals. New York: Quorum Books, 1992.
3. Arnaldo, Carlos A. ed. Child Abuse on the Internet: Ending the Silence. New York: Berghahn Books, 2001.
4. Braiker, Harriet B. The Disease to Please. McGraw Hill, 2001.
5. Brant, Renee. Case Vignette: Child Abuse or Acceptable Cultural Norms. Ethics & Behavior. 5 No. 3 (1995): 283.
6. Cahill, Ann J. Rethinking Rape. New York: Cornell University Press, 2001.
7. Callaway, Allison. Deaf Children in China. Washington: Gallaudet University Press, 2000.
8. Dances With Wolves, Kevin Costner. Tig Productions, 1990.
9. Davis, Kimberly. Making Blended Families Work, Ebony 55, No. 12 (October 2000): 40.
10. Escher, Ursula. Self-Defense for Kids. Pak's Karate Studio, 2003.
11. Feltham, Colin and Windy Dryden. Brief Counseling: A Practical, Integrative Approach. England: Open University Press, 2006.
12. Forrest Gump, Robert Zemeckis. Paramount Pictures, 1994.
13. Galpin, Timothy J. and Mark Herndon. The Complete Guide to Mergers and Acquisitions: Process Tools to Support M&A Integration at Every Level. San Francisco: Jossey-Bass, 2000.
14. Gladwell, Malcolm. The Tipping Point. New York: Little Brown and Company, 2000, 2001.
15. Konzak, Burt and Melina and Sonya Konzak. Girl Power. Canada: Sports Book Publisher, 1999.
16. Lamar, Donna F. Transcending Turmoil: Survivors of Dysfunctional Families. New York: Plenum Press, 1992.

17. La Torre, Mary Anne. Meditation and Psychotherapy: An Effective Combination. Perspectives in Psychiatric Care 37 (2001): 1.
18. Levinson, Harry. The Great Jackass Fallacy. Cambridge: Harvard University Press, 1973.
19. Lewis, Michael. The Man Who Crashed the World, Vanity Fair (August 2009): 98.
20. McGraw's Search for His Father, The Week (November 13, 2009): 10.
21. Miller, John P. The Contemplative Practitioner: Meditation in Education and the Professions. Connecticut: Bergin & Garvey, 1994.
22. Mitroff, Ian I. Managing Crises Before They Happen: What Every Executive and Manager Needs to Know About Crisis Management. New York: Amacon, 2001.
23. Norment, Lynn. What's Behind the Dramatic Rise in Rapes? Ebony 44, no. 11 (September 1991): 92.
24. Peled, Einat, Zvi Eisikovits, Guy Enosh, and Zeev Winstok. Choice and Empowerment for Battered Women Who Stay: Toward a Constructivist Model. Social Work 45, No. 1 (2000): 9.
25. Pickering W.S.F. and Geoffrey Walford. Durkheim's Suicide: A Century of Research and Debate. United Kingdom: Routledge 2000.
26. Pray the Devil Back To Hell, Abigail E. Disney and Gini Reticker. Fork Films, 2008.
27. Raines, Clare and Lara Ewing. The Art of Connecting: How to Overcome Differences, Build Rapport, and Communicate Effectively With Anyone. New York: Amacon, 2006.
28. Radford, Benjamin. Predator Panic: A Closer Look, Skeptical Inquirer 30, (September 2006): 1.
29. Ray, Taylor Hackford. Bristol Bay Productions, 2004.
30. Robinson, Duke. Too Nice for Your Own Good. New York: Warner Books, 1997.
31. Rubin, Harriet. The Power of Words, Fast Company, January 1999. http://www.fastcompany.com/magazine/21/flores.html.
32. Sanderson, Christiane. Counseling Adult Survivors of Child Sexual Abuse. London: Jessica Kingsley, 2006.
33. Searle, John R. Speech Acts: An Essay in the Philosophy of Language. Cambridge, Cambridge University Press, 1969.
34. Skowron, Elizabeth A., Stephen R. Wester, and Razia Azen. Differentiation of Self Mediates College Stress and Adjustment. Journal of Counseling and Development 84, No. 1 (2004): 69.

35. Smith, Manual J. When I Say No, I Feel Guilty. Bantam Books, 1975.
36. South Park, Trey Parker and Matt Stone. Comedy Central, 1997-2010.
37. Strauss, Kandra. Dumping the Stress by Getting Fit, National Education Association 20, No. 7 (April 2002): 35.
38. Talking Heads. Once in a Lifetime on Remain in Light (audio CD). Burbank, California: Distributed by Warner Brothers/Wea, 1980.
39. The Miracle Worker, Arthur Penn. Playfilm Productions, 1962.
40. Verbatim, Time, February 2, 2009, 20.
41. Wallerstein, Judith S. and Joan B. Kelly. Surviving the Breakup: How Children and Parents Cope With Divorce. New York: Basic Books, 1966.
42. Winkler, Karen. Kinsey, Sex Research, and the Body of Knowledge: Let's Talk about Sex. Women's Studies Quarterly 33, (2005): 285.
43. Zusne, Leonard, and Warren H. Jones. Anomalistic Psychology: A Study of Magical Thinking. New Jersey: Lawrence Erlbaum Associates, 1989.